Restoring Our Bodies, Reclaiming Our Lives

Restoring Our Bodies, Reclaiming Our Lives

Guidance and Reflections on Recovery
from Eating Disorders

EDITED AND WITH AN INTRODUCTION BY
AIMEE LIU

*Foreword by Judith D. Banker,
Past President, Academy for Eating Disorders*

Trumpeter
Boston & London
2011

Trumpeter Books
An imprint of Shambhala Publications, Inc.
Horticultural Hall
300 Massachusetts Avenue
Boston, Massachusetts 02115
www.shambhala.com

9 8 7 6 5 4 3 2 1

First Edition
Printed in the United States of America

♾ This edition is printed on acid-free paper that meets
the American National Standards Institute z39.48 Standard.
♻ This book was printed on 30% postconsumer recycled paper.
For more information please visit www.shambhala.com.

Distributed in the United States by Random House, Inc.,
and in Canada by Random House of Canada Ltd

Designed by Lora Zorian

Library of Congress Cataloging-in-Publication Data

Restoring our bodies, reclaiming our lives: guidance and
reflections on recovery from eating disorders / edited and
with an introduction by Aimee Liu; foreword by Judith D. Banker.
p.   cm.
Includes bibliographical references.
ISBN 978-1-59030-877-6 (pbk.: alk. paper)
1. Eating disorders—Psychological aspects.
2. Eating disorders—Patients—Biography. I. Liu, Aimee.
RC552.E18R523 2011
616.85'26—dc22
2010038488

Contents

Foreword

NOT ONE PATIENT I'VE EVER TREATED for an eating disorder believed at the outset of treatment that she or he was capable of recovering. Not a single one could imagine being free of the relentless obsessing, the perpetual weight-loss algorithms, the self-loathing, shame, or despair that accompany these excruciatingly complex and devastating illnesses. Yet, despite their doubts, the majority of people with eating disorders do recover. How does that happen? What makes it possible to recover from an eating disorder? What takes place during the recovery process, and what does it feel like to be recovered? Are there ways to help the process along?

Eating-disorder researchers and practitioners are studying these and other questions in order to identify the best treatments and opportunities for recovery. We have learned that access to appropriate levels of specialized care, a strong alliance with treatment providers, and supportive relationships with family and friends can have a positive impact on recovery. In addition, research trials have shown certain therapies to be especially useful with younger patients and with particular types of eating disorders. This is a start. But it's a far cry from the range of definitive answers we need in order to ensure recovery for every person who seeks help for an eating disorder. While the majority of people do recover, there are still many who remain disabled by eating disorders. Far too many lose their lives to these illnesses. And too many families are severely challenged by the financial and emotional demands of finding effective care for their loved ones. We need to learn more about who recovers and why, and about what challenges and experiences people can expect as they engage in the recovery process.

The myriad personal reflections of people who've recovered from eating disorders, along with their loved ones' perspectives, can help us learn to ask the critical research and clinical questions. In *Restoring Our Bodies, Reclaiming Our Lives,* Aimee Liu has amassed a rich amalgam of human experience and added the professional expertise of members of the global Academy for Eating Disorders (AED) to provide deep insight into the recovery process. Here readers will find information about the tools and interventions that research, clinical knowledge, and personal experience have proven can help people recover.

In her last book, *Gaining: The Truth about Life after Eating Disorders,* Aimee used the expert interweaving of scientific and clinical understanding of eating disorders with the reality of personal experience to create a powerful, layered, and unflinching portrayal of life beyond recovery. *Gaining* is essential reading for people seeking recovery and for their families and friends, as well as for eating-disorder professionals. In *Restoring Our Bodies, Reclaiming Our Lives* Aimee again joins the wisdom of personal experience and the knowledge of research and clinical experts to provide a keenly illuminating, in-depth journey into the recovery process.

Most books address recovery as a postscript between the ravages of the eating-disorder experience and life "happily ever after." *Restoring Our Bodies, Reclaiming Our Lives* forges new ground by walking the reader through the entire recovery process, from the initial turning points at the start of the odyssey to the "wise minds" that reflect on the experience of reclaiming one's life after an eating disorder.

Illnesses as complicated as eating disorders, which arise from and influence multiple mental, emotional, physical, and social systems, are not easily explained or understood. Paradoxically, their complexity makes eating disorders prone to oversimplification. People with eating disorders are often mistakenly judged to be self-indulgent, self-absorbed, or manipulative. They may be told that they lack willpower or are just trying to get attention; frequently their families are tagged as the cause of the problem. This stigmatization prevents individuals and health systems from taking eating disorders seriously and can impede early intervention and critical access to specialized care.

The Academy for Eating Disorders (AED) owes Aimee a debt of gratitude for the countless hours she has dedicated to the writing of this book and for her inspiring and generous gift of the book's royalties to the AED. A global multidisciplinary professional association, the AED is dedicated to promoting the highest-quality eating-disorders research, education, treatment, and prevention. The AED wholeheartedly supports innovative efforts to educate the public and the professional communities about eating disorders. The expert commentaries in this book, for example, were contributed by AED researchers and practitioners with specialties in those topic areas.

Through Aimee's generosity and dedication to the field, the royalties from the sales of *Restoring Our Bodies, Reclaiming Our Lives* will go to the AED Clinical and Research Scholarship Fund. This program provides annual scholarships to support the education and training of outstanding professionals from underserved regions of the world. These individuals in return bring this valuable information and training back to their communities, improving the quality and accessibility of eating-disorders research and treatment worldwide. Aimee's donation will expand the reach of this essential program.

As the number of people around the world suffering from eating, weight, and body-image disorders continues to grow, we rely on authors of Aimee Liu's caliber to tell the personal, the therapeutic, and the scientific truth about these illnesses. *Restoring Our Bodies, Reclaiming Our Lives* is an important new contribution to our knowledge base about eating disorders. It is also an invaluable guide that will inspire, reassure, and support those seeking their own recovery.

JUDITH D. BANKER, MA, LLP, FAED
Past President, Academy for Eating Disorders (AED)

Introduction

Hi.

My name is Anouska, I'm twenty, live in Western Australia, and was diagnosed with anorexia last year. I've been out of the clinic for over a month and I'm faced with the possibility of a second admission.

I don't know what I am hoping for by e-mailing you—I won't be surprised if I never gain a response—but I find it so hard to believe that people do recover. That the voice does go away, that the all-consuming desire for thinness disappears, and the nonexistent self-worth somehow rediscovers its feet. I have read many recovery books: from the first chapter—"I only ate xyz a day," "I weighed xxx pounds"—to the last—"I've now been recovered for five years," "it's an ongoing process, it was difficult but I got there"—no details about how they recovered! It's so disheartening.

Maybe recovery is possible; but maybe it's just not possible for me.

God Bless,

—*Anouska*

Dear Anouska,

I agree with you that many eating-disorder memoirs do leave out the vital details of recovery, and that can be frustrating. I write about self-awareness and try to focus on the process of recovery. It's not about dieting or weight. I have recovered, and the vast majority of people with eating disorders do recover. If you've been ill for a long time, it will take some time to retrain your brain. But with the help of a good therapist you really can free yourself from ED's domination.

You need to understand, though, that an eating disorder is a distress signal, and you need to confront the real source of distress and find constructive ways to confront and manage that conflict. This includes marshaling the courage to change.

Perfection is an illusion. Humans are imperfect. Life involves joy and love as well as suffering. Those are just a few of the truths I've learned to embrace. Truth can be incredibly liberating.

Please be well and patient and compassionate with yourself. Accept—demand!—the help you need to recover now.

—Aimee

The letters began to flood my inbox even before the release of my book *Gaining: The Truth about Life after Eating Disorders.* Women who'd heard me on the radio, or attended a discussion group, or caught one of my television interviews wrote to tell me their stories of suffering, struggling, and, in many cases, recovering from anorexia, bulimia, and binge-eating disorders. Some wrote to ask my advice. Parents wrote for solace. Husbands wrote to express the toll an eating disorder takes on intimacy. Over and over and over I heard, "I've never told these things to anyone else. I'm writing because I know you understand."

There was also a recurrent question that emerged, both in the letters and in the responses of audience members at talks I gave across the country: "What is it like to recover?" People desperately wanted to know not only how they could—or "should"—recover but also, and perhaps even more urgently, what their experience of recovery would feel and look like.

In a multitude of ways, eating disorders express anxiety. If you have a history of anorexia, for example, you're likely sensitive and perfectionistic. When ill, you not only exaggerate the rightness or wrongness of numbers on the scale, but you may also imagine there's a right way and a wrong way to recover. Recovery's promise of change and potential for failure may loom as terrifying threats. Jessie, a young woman six months into treatment, described this beautifully when she wrote, "Recovery is a process and a unique journey for each person; I think that message needs to be shared more often, and can be a message of comfort for all those perfectionistic people in the midst of recovery who feel they are not recovering in the perfect way."

Many of the people Jessie alluded to have proven to themselves that they're "good at" eating disorders. With food restriction, they may experience a hunger high. With purging, they may go numb. With binge eating, they may zone out. Eventually, having dedicated their very identity to ED (pronounced "Ed," the name many sufferers give to the enslaving voice that eating disorders plant in their brains; and the name by which I'll refer to that voice throughout this book), many no longer know how to recognize, much less sustain, healthy relationships or more rewarding pursuits. This radical distortion of self-worth effectively enslaves an individual to ED. For young women like Anouska, who are in the grip of their illness, health can seem an impossible goal.

Yet the majority of letters I've received prove both that recovery *is* possible and that it *must* be different for everyone. While people who are gravely ill with an eating disorder often bear an alarming resemblance to each other, those who recover do so, in large part, by exploring their own unique ways of talking, acting, thinking, feeling, and looking—both *at* themselves and *to* the world.

This can be disturbing news to those who cling to a single rigid standard of perfection, who are so fearful of making a mistake that they dare not entertain more authentic and promising dreams. But fear thrives in the abstract. The concrete example of individuals who've moved through and beyond an eating disorder beats back fear by engendering hope.

Instead of balking at the overwhelming complexity and uncertainty of life after eating disorders, those who have hope begin to imagine themselves striking out, making free choices, and discovering their true appetites. As conversations about recovery deepen, so does the sense of personal possibility. I've witnessed this change often in my correspondences with readers over the past few years.

As a novelist, I'm well aware of the power of stories to surprise and inspire change. But stories that tell the truth with genuine emotional honesty are also, quite simply, fascinating. The letters I've received are rich with insights that push far beyond the forty-odd life stories that informed *Gaining*. By the hundreds, they support my contention that eating disorders are like a gun that's formed by genetics, loaded by culture and family ideals, and triggered by unbearable distress. However, the letters bear out this metaphor with stunningly unpredictable examples.

One letter described a woman with an eating disorder who's never seen a fashion magazine and has no idea what Mary Kate Olsen or Nicole Richie looks like. Why not? Because she's been blind since birth. Another recounted how the shock of change can trigger relapse: "After pregnancy had, I thought, cured me of eating disorders, mine resurfaced shortly after Hurricane Katrina. I stopped eating when it became clear that we were going to be displaced for a while, and I lost more than ten pounds during the six weeks of our evacuation in Houston. Many things I thought were completely unrelated to my food issues are connected." Several letters contained family histories of eating disorders that began with grandfathers who continued restrictive eating patterns after being forced to starve during the Holocaust. Others traced the patterns of weight-obsession to fathers and brothers who were bodybuilders and wrestlers. One woman realized in the course of our correspondence that, when she was little, her father used to excuse himself every night during their after-dinner walks to vomit by the side of the road; his eating disorder was never diagnosed, but she'd been struggling with hers for years and only now connected the dots.

Because *Gaining* focused primarily on recovery from anorexia and bulimia, most of the letters initially came from readers with histories of restricting and purging. But as I began to blog and write other articles on the wider range of eating disorders, I received notes from people who struggled with binge eating and other varieties of eating disorders. My correspondents were all ages and from all over the world. The majority of letters came from women. In part, this reflects the fact that 75 percent of those who struggle with eating disorders are women. In part, it reflects the fact that men are more likely to go undiagnosed and untreated. Another reason may well be that because I'm female, male readers were less willing to confide in me than women were. That said, I was struck by the number of men acknowledged in the letters, either as supportive family members or as fellow sufferers. Although the letters described recovery from a female perspective, it was clear that recovery is not exclusively a female journey.

The breadth and depth of these letters demanded that I compile them in a form that could benefit others. *Restoring Our Bodies, Reclaiming Our Lives* is the result. This compilation traces the course of recovery from those who've recently reached their turning point and begun to seek help to those ten, twenty, or thirty years well. In their own words, those who have sought and gained true health profile what recovery looks like.

Shannon, a twenty-two-year-old just beginning intensive treatment for her eating disorder, echoed many when she agreed to participate in this project: "I think a book of letters would be so helpful for everyone, from those completely isolated by ED to those individuals less controlled but nonetheless influenced. It would be so therapeutic to literally read along through the stages of recovery. And personally, it would make me much more optimistic in my path toward recovery, truly knowing that it was possible."

Many also expressed another motive for allowing me to reprint their notes. Kate, a twenty-nine-year-old wife and mother from Oregon who'd battled eating disorders since she was eight, wrote, "If it can help even one person to know that she's not alone, it's worth it. I would be honored for you to use my letter." There's power both in helping others and in voicing the truth. This power is one of the strongest antidotes to mental illness, so by sharing their letters in this book, I realized, each contributor was also helping herself.

But publishing these letters also serves a further purpose. As I was researching *Gaining*, I discovered the enormous strides science is making both to identify the root causes of and to develop effective treatments for eating disorders. We now know that, globally, millions of people of every age, class, race, and culture suffer from these biologically based mental illnesses. All eating disorders can be fatal, and the longer they persist, the more damage they do to mind, body, and spirit. Eating disorders have a higher mortality rate than schizophrenia, alcoholism, or depression. Yet eating disorders receive only a fraction of the research funding that goes to these other conditions. And in most regions of the world, private insurance and government funding for treatment are not adequate to support the specialized care required to cure these illnesses. Why? The answer, in a word, is *stigma*.

The stigma that surrounds eating disorders paints them as trivial "girl problems," diets gone awry, adolescent rites of passage, or the acting out of juvenile rebels or "control freaks." Anorexia, bulimia, and binge-eating disorders are sensationalized by the media as celebrity spectacles. Even the medical profession, by and large, still dismisses disordered eating as a behavioral quirk and thus fails to recognize the serious psychological threat this behavior represents. Stigma suppresses funding and attention to eating-disorders research and is a primary obstacle to adequate treatment and prevention efforts.

In 2008 I joined the advisory board of the Academy for Eating Disorders to help fight the stigma and promote scientific research on eating disorders. All net royalties from *Restoring Our Bodies, Reclaiming Our Lives* will be donated to the AED's research scholarship fund.

The Academy for Eating Disorders, in return, has worked with me to make this book a comprehensive resource with expert advice on issues such as treatment, insurance coverage, and options for concerned family members as well as for those suffering from eating disorders.

The letters that follow tell the truth about recovery as no single story or conventional self-help book can. It's a truth as varied and complex as eating disorders themselves, and as powerful as the human spirit. So take heart. Read on. And know that you, too, have the right and the power to thrive.

WORDS

Words on paper;
my thoughts,
my ideas,
my voice.
Once written down
they are said,
confirmed,
and acknowledged.

My words stare back at me,
like my reflection in
the mirror.
Instead of showing
the form of my body,
or the color of my skin.
My words on paper
reveal my soul
and spirit within.

—SARA DUNCAN

ONE

Turning Points

VIRTUALLY ALL THE PEOPLE I've ever met who've recovered from an eating disorder can recall the particular moment when they first turned onto the road back to health. Whether they thought it, felt it, heard it, or read it, they knew in that instant that they'd had *enough*! Enough hunger. Enough isolation, pain, and fear. Enough acting out of shame and emptiness for one lifetime and then some.

This moment is never a cure-all epiphany—recovery *always* takes time—but the turning point is nonetheless crucially significant. It marks the end of ED's absolute tyranny over the self, a declaration (if not yet the realization) of independence, and the beginning of true self-awareness. However brief or fleeting it may seem, this shift represents a vital transfer of power from compulsion to free choice.

The particulars of the turning point are different for every individual, but they often require two seemingly opposite emotional ingredients: acute distress and hope. Hope without distress only tends to perpetuate the illusion that an eating disorder will resolve on its own; and distress without hope only intensifies the despair that already surrounds the illness. Fortunately, there are as many sources of hope in the world as there are causes of distress. And when we are most in need, we often pay attention to signals that otherwise would pass us by.

I recently received a note from a young woman whose first confrontation with the reality of death—losing her beloved grandfather—told her she did not want to go where her eating disorder was leading her. Others have confided that their turning points came when they had to choose between obeying ED and nourishing their love for a partner, a child, or even a pet—and love won. Still others have been inspired by more ephemeral forces—a transcendent moment of faith or a glimpse of beauty or purpose so profound that it rendered senseless their drive toward darkness, and allowed them to imagine life without ED.

The road to recovery may be lined with false turns, but once you've hit a true turning point, you can't mistake it. What distinguishes such moments is their stark emotional authenticity. Whether yours leaves you feeling shaken to your knees or ignited from within, the experience will compel you to leave your death march for the journey back to health.

Becky: If Not Now, When?

Becky, now a senior in college, was eleven years old when she entered what she describes as her "bunker of restriction," otherwise known as ED. Friends, teachers, and family spotted trouble and began reaching out to her in sixth grade. But it wasn't until her second semester of college that she reached her true turning point. The moment outwardly resembled thousands of others over the course of her disease. But inside that moment, a critical shift began.

WHEN I WAS YOUNG, I was tentative and anxious, concerned that my academic performance, athletic skills, musical talent, body size, and level of devotion as a daughter were never good enough. When these fears became overwhelming and uncontrollable, my eating disorder led me to an emotionally reclusive and hidden state. Like a dormant seed refusing to blossom because of the harsh conditions of the outside world, I hunkered down in my bunker of restriction, purging and over-exercising for my own long, cold winter.

Looking back, it's hard for me to believe that I had any conscious understanding of what I was doing. But I do know that it didn't feel like a choice. It was the only way I could be spared my disgust and dissatisfaction with myself. I didn't want to accept the help that I needed. I lied and deceived my parents, caregivers, and friends. Instead of taking responsibility, I'd create artificial deadlines to be "finished with my eating disorder"—whatever that meant. My first "deadline" was the end of eighth grade and, like many that would follow, was not met.

I fell into a pattern. I'd enter treatment, stabilize on the premise of a false deadline, and then fall apart, restarting the whole cycle. But I truly believed I wanted to get better, and managed to convince my parents and my treatment team that I was ready to leave home to begin college.

Freshman year I started to catch glimpses of health, of blossoming. I made a group of friends, became involved in student organizations, and met my wonderful boyfriend. Despite all these accomplishments, soon after returning for second semester, I found myself again ensnared in my eating disorder. I kept myself secluded, too tired, cold, and anxious to experience the wonderful things that a college student should. As the semester passed me by, my therapist and medical doctor began suggesting that I withdraw for the semester to seek treatment. I told them this was giving up and I was going to finish the year. I did indeed finish the year with straight A's, but I came home depleted, depressed, and desperate.

A few days after I returned I stepped on a scale. This activity that for so long was either characterized by excessive checking or intense phobia served as a major reality check. It triggered a set of emotions that I hadn't let myself feel for many years. The idea of "what if . . . . . . I was healthy, happy, content" suddenly became questions that I no longer could ignore.

I didn't know if I wanted to get better, but I knew I had to give myself a chance to bring my body to a place where it could appropriately make that decision. In my current state, I didn't have the capacity to choose health. For the first time, I entered a residential program with a real willingness to listen to my doctors and, more importantly, listen to what was deep inside of me, a little tiny glimmer of hope.

Now, I'm not one to use quotes to express my emotions, but a quote of Rabbi Hillel's, one of the most influential scholars in Jewish history, started to enter my mind around this time. Hillel said, "If I am not for myself, then who will be for me? And if I am only for myself, then what am I? And if not now, when?" The quote has often been used to describe the history of the Jewish people and to motivate young Jewish minds, but it had and continues to have an undeniable connection to my recovery. These simple questions awakened emotions and thoughts that I'd refused to let myself feel for years.

My residential stay was not easy. I made many teary phone calls saying that I was going to sign myself out of the program and that I just couldn't take the stress of the weight gain and intensive therapy. Despite these feelings, something deep inside would not let me leave the program. I knew that I had to give myself a shot at health, a chance to grow up and out. Once my body was physically healthier and my mind clearer, I could then decide whether or not I truly wanted to get better. And I knew that if I didn't give myself this option now, I was bound to live a miserable life, a life with an eating disorder.

With each day of nourishment, I became stronger both physically and mentally. I faced Rabbi Hillel's questions with a little bit more hope than I had on the previous day. When I was discharged, I had a feeling that I'd never experienced upon leaving a program. I sensed and began to feel the possibilities of life. "If not now, when?" For the first time, I felt comfortable answering, "Now!"

This discharge was just over two years ago. Please don't be mistaken; these two years have not been easy. I've worked each day to win small battles with myself over my own self-worth. But something is different now. I'm winning these battles. I'm choosing my health and my future, two concepts that were so foreign to me only a few short years ago. I've decided I no longer want a life of restriction. I've traded it in for a full life.

I nourish myself each and every day, and as a result, I can walk down the street on a crisp fall day and feel the contrast of the warm sun with the cool air on my face, and I feel content. I can walk through a museum and experience beauty and think of nothing else. My boyfriend of two and half years has shown me that it's safe to love and be loved, and that has allowed me to slowly break away from the scars of my past. I also experience spirituality in a new way. My Judaism, previously bound by prayer books and long hours in temple, has been a guiding light in my process. Jewish values and emphasis on the importance of life have had an immense impact on me.

At the end of the day, I want recovery because I've grown to enjoy the feeling of contentedness, happiness, and health. Of course, there will be darker days here and there, but I've chosen the path of health, and I have no intention of turning back.

How and When?
The Ingredients of Change
By Josie Geller

There is a palpable distinction that's felt when a person embarks wholeheartedly on the recovery process and develops passion for life without ED. How can you—or your loved ones—tell when you're ready for recovery? Although no one can say exactly when the turning point will come, researchers recently have been studying the factors associated with increases in readiness to change, and some of these are highlighted in Becky's letter:

1. *Turning away from numbers as a measure of self-worth*

Initially, Becky judged her success by rigid external standards, such as grades and numbers on the scale. Without more personally gratifying or meaningful ways of valuing herself, she developed a habit of self-criticism. She cut herself off from others, and her eating disorder lingered. Recognizing that the number on the scale did not produce happiness can be an important first step on the path to recovery.

2. *Building relationships with others*

Becky began to recover a truer sense of herself when she opened up her life to include a broader array of activities. She joined student organizations, became involved in a significant intimate relationship, and discovered new ways to experience meaning and emotion. Rabbi Hillel's invitation to contemplate self-direction and the preciousness of time also seemed to help Becky become more mindful of physical experiences, of the value of safety and intimacy in human interactions, and of her Jewish faith. Her ability to live in the moment and practice self-compassion helped in this transformation.

3. Connecting with a higher purpose

Research has shown that meaningful, long-lasting change begins when we discover more compelling and fulfilling alternatives to our current circumstances. Connecting with a higher purpose for Becky involved focusing less on external achievements and finding greater fulfillment in connection to others. Although the specifics vary from individual to individual, finding a higher purpose is often associated with feeling less distress, more confidence, less preoccupation with body shape and weight, and greater openness to embarking on change. The good news is that discovering a higher purpose benefits individuals at all stages of recovery.

Steve: Man Enough

Steve took a long time reaching his turning point, in part because he was not female, and in part because he was an athlete. Many people still assume that boys and men can't develop eating disorders, even though a 2007 Harvard study found that men account for 40 percent of binge eaters and nearly 25 percent of people who struggle with restricting and purging behavior. Many of these men are athletes in sports such as wrestling, bodybuilding, horseracing, running, and cycling and surfing—Steve's sports—which place a premium on leanness.

Today Steve has a master's degree in exercise science, works as a renal dietitian, and offers the kind of sports-nutrition consulting that he wishes had been available to him back when he dreamed of becoming a professional cyclist like Lance Armstrong. He'd read that Armstrong weighed and measured his food and that Armstrong's competitor Jan Ullrich lost the Tour de France because he'd gained weight during the off-season. In Steve's mind, less weight equaled greater speed, so he began to "train like a horse and eat like a rabbit." But Steve was already struggling with anorexia when he became a competitive athlete. The rigors of his sport only accelerated his illness. Finally Steve decided he'd had enough of ED.

I FELT LIKE MY BODY was eating itself. My parents already knew. They saw my bones through my shirts; they saw the sunken look in my face, but they could not make it any better. No one could make me want to get better . . . without my own drive it wasn't going to happen.

Being a male with a "female's" disease was so disheartening. There was no relating; no connecting, no nothing. The disease tears everything away from you. You lose friends. You lose the ability to think clearly.

I'd been to therapists. One looked at me and asked, "So why don't you just eat?" I couldn't communicate starving and over-exercising; they weren't getting it . . . no one was.

My loves of surfing and cycling were definitely affected. Cycling was something that fueled and repressed my struggles with the eating disorder. In the beginning stages, cycling and all forms of exercise were used as penance for eating or for any emotions I was feeling. Surfing was something that, at the height of my struggles with food and exercise, I could not do; I'd try to experience the bliss that I'd felt on the water ever since I began surfing at eleven, but my body would get too weak and cold . . . even in the middle of the summer in 80-degree water. Exercise and burning calories was the main goal, and in my mind surfing was not fulfilling those criteria, so I did without this one and only thing that truly gave me satisfaction, friendships, and self-confidence.

I can clearly remember being alone in my parents' living room, pacing because I was so hungry. My body was crying out with pain from places I never thought could produce pain. I was thinking, "This isn't fun. Why am I doing this to myself? I don't deserve this."

From that day on I searched for the right treatment and found a therapist and dietitian who led me in the beginning stages of recovery. My therapist held no presumptions, was unbiased and genuine. She showed empathy, knowing that young men with eating disorders don't have the same resources as girls and women. She never pushed me farther than we both knew I could go, while still challenging me and supporting me when I needed it most.

ED'S MEN
What's Different about Male Eating Disorders
By Tom Hildebrandt

Like their female counterparts, men and boys with eating disorders come in all shapes and sizes. And in males as in females, ED often hides behind the pursuit of athletic achievement, health, and/or perfect appearance. But among males with ED, physical ideals can vary substantially from person to person. Some boys and men want to be thinner, but others develop eating disorders while bodybuilding or pursuing the lean muscularity of an underwear model. Still others become intent on achieving a particular level of physical fitness, with no special body shape or size in mind.

Because men's physical goals are so varied, eating-disordered behavior among males can range from starvation to purposeful overeating, from purging to anabolic-androgenic steroid abuse. This diversity of symptoms has helped to perpetuate the myth that males don't have eating disorders, which in turn poses a major obstacle to the prevention, diagnosis, and treatment of ED in males.

Other obstacles that can prevent males from seeking help and recovering include the following:

- *Stigma.* The notion that eating disorders "belong" to women and girls can make it difficult for males to admit they have this problem. Many men also believe it's not "manly" to seek out or accept professional help. Clinicians may inadvertently reinforce these cultural attitudes if they fail to diagnose eating-disorder symptoms in males or if they don't refer them for therapy. This bias may also prevent friends and family from intervening as quickly with a male showing ED symptoms as they would with a female.
- *Sexuality.* It's also widely and incorrectly assumed that eating disorders in men reflect their sexual preference. As a result, adolescent and adult males may fear that if they admit to having an eating disorder, their sexuality will be questioned. This anxiety may prevent them from seeking treatment. In fact, men of all sexual preferences can develop these disorders.

- *Access to treatment.* Males who are able to overcome these initial hurdles may face a final, even more imposing challenge when they seek a therapist who will treat them. Many ED treatment providers and programs focus their services on females. Even if they do treat males, access to group therapy or support groups can be limited, or a patient might find himself the lone male in a group of female patients. Fortunately, treatment services that address the unique needs of males with ED are becoming increasingly available. The organizations listed in the Resources section at the back of this book can recommend available programs in your area.

If you're male and are struggling with an eating disorder, take steps now to get the help you really need. It will give you your best chance of recovery!

Kim: Hearing the Truth

Kim has been free of her eating disorder for twenty-five years, but she still vividly remembers how many turning points she missed, ignored, or denied before she was willing to face the truth.

EVERY DAY THE SAME. Living two lives. Outwardly, going to classes, to work, going home, hanging out with friends. Sure, the food I ate was different, but I could pass as a health food nut or vegetarian. Sure, I was skinny, but it was genetic, right? It was what nobody saw, what was in my mind that made me different. The obsession—the relentless, ruthless rhythm of the drive for thinness that would never leave me alone. Every store window, every fashion magazine, every thin woman reminded me. My brain had become a computer, programmed to persistently install new updates that would enable me to more effectively serve the god of thinness embodied in the scale.

The first turning point: "Here, read this." My now ex-boyfriend handed me an article as he walked out the door. Shocked by the title, "Anorexia Nervosa," I threw it in the garbage. Twenty minutes later I retrieved it and devoured it just like I'd devoured potato skins from the trash. "That's not me!" Yet, I knew it was.

The second turning point: "To get well demands a new, greater sacrifice—namely, giving up this unnatural pride in something that doesn't accomplish anything!" Dr. Hilde Bruch's words stung as though she had reached out from the pages of her book and slapped me across the face. She was talking about the relentless pursuit of thinness. I read *The Golden Cage* into the wee hours of the morning, hating the words but unable to draw myself away. I knew she was right.

The third turning point: " . . . of eternal value." These were the words I added to Dr. Bruch's proclamation about the meaninglessness of being skinny. All my time and energy was spent in the pursuit of something that made no contribution to the world and had no spiritual significance. I professed a strong faith in God, but I worshipped the scale. This incongruity grated on my nerves. I still didn't change my behavior.

The fourth turning point: I didn't understand why [my friend] was staring at me like I was a creature from another planet. It was so normal to me, the food I was eating, the exercise routine I compulsively followed, the rigid schedule that supported my day like a skeleton holds up a body. I'd even gained some weight. "I just can't get close to you," she said. "It's like you won't bend. It's the food thing." I just stared at her, tears and anger welling up. Why can't she just accept me as I am? That's what we're all supposed to do for each other, right? Yet I knew she spoke the truth.

The fifth turning point: "You are still too thin." Because it was my father and boyfriend speaking, the words pierced my denial. Because it was my father and boyfriend speaking, my hackles went up immediately. I'd already gained so much weight and worked so hard, and still it wasn't enough! Yet I knew they spoke the truth.

After reading *The Golden Cage,* I made the decision that I would not live the rest of my life as an anorexic. I didn't want the epitaph on my tombstone to read, "We will always remember her eating disorder." I wanted to be remembered for more than that. Just like Dorothy setting out on the yellow brick road, I was determined not to stop until I reached my goal of recovery.

Labeling ED
What Are the Different Types of Eating Disorders?
By Susan J. Paxton

Eating disorders take many different forms and have many different causes, but all can have devastating consequences for sufferers and their family and friends. Anorexia nervosa and bulimia nervosa are the best-known eating disorders, but clinicians also recognize other serious illnesses such as binge eating disorder (BED) and symptom patterns that are included in a general category known as eating disorders not otherwise specified (EDNOS).

The eating disorder that attracts the most media attention is anorexia nervosa, although in fact it is the least common disorder. Anorexia is characterized by a relentless pursuit of thinness resulting in a very low weight and, in girls and women, loss of menstrual periods. The key symptom of this illness is severe food restriction. Sometimes the restriction is accompanied by excessive exercise or activity and other behaviors that are attempts to compensate for any food consumed. Severe body-image disturbances are also a key feature of anorexia.

It is estimated that less than half of one percent of girls over the age of fifteen years suffer from anorexia. Although it is often associated with teenage or young women, this illness can affect anyone of any age, including men and older adults. As can be seen in the stories in this book, the psychological and relationship effects of this disorder, as well as the physical effects associated with starvation, are devastating. They may last many years and can be life threatening. However, it is important to remember that the majority of people affected by anorexia nervosa do recover and can tell remarkable stories of bravery and triumph.

Bulimia nervosa is characterized by frequent binge eating followed by some form of compensation for bingeing, such as extreme dieting, excessive exercise, self-induced vomiting, or laxative misuse. Severe body dissatisfaction and self-disparagement are also distressing parts of this disorder. In contrast to anorexia, people affected by bulimia are generally at or above a healthy weight. As eating-disordered behavior usually occurs in private and symptoms are not obvious to an observer, the painful and destructive nature of bulimia is sometimes underestimated. In fact, the death rate from bulimia—about 4 percent of those diagnosed—is similar to that of anorexia. Fortunately, treatment can be very helpful for people with bulimia.

Binge Eating Disorder (BED) is another common eating disorder. BED is characterized by frequent binge eating and feelings of being out of control with food, though the individual does not physically try to compensate for the food eaten during a binge. Some, but not all people with BED, carry extra weight as a result of bingeing episodes.

Eating-disorder symptoms rarely fit neatly into a particular category, so Eating Disorder Not Otherwise Specified (EDNOS) is a diagnosis that includes eating patterns that resemble anorexia nervosa or bulimia nervosa but do not exactly match the profile of those illnesses. Many, if not most, people in treatment for an eating disorder have symptoms that fall under the diagnosis of EDNOS. Symptoms often change through the course of recovery. For example, someone with bulimia may be able to stop purging before she is able to stop bingeing. So, for a time, her symptoms may resemble BED rather than bulimia. Or someone with anorexia who also purges could go through a period of time where she is eating more normally but has not resumed menses or stopped purging. Because she is not restricting her food, her symptoms would no longer fit under the diagnosis of anorexia nervosa but would fit under EDNOS.

These distinctions can be useful for researchers who must strictly control the parameters in their studies or for clinicians who need to determine treatment directions. However, for people in recovery who are moving through different phases and different symptom patterns, the distinctions may be of limited value. The most important point to note is that EDNOS is not a milder form of anorexia or bulimia nervosa; it is simply a different manifestation of an eating disorder. *All* eating disorders are serious illnesses with profound physical and emotional consequences.

Jessie: Recognizing the Power to Change

I've been honored to learn that my own words have helped some readers reach their turning point. When Gaining *was published, I was interviewed on the U.S. radio station National Public Radio about the discoveries I'd made while researching the book. Jessie is a young woman who was listening that day.*

I VIVIDLY RECALL the cold afternoon last winter as I was sitting in my kitchen, preparing my lunch and debating whether or not I "deserved" to put almonds in with my tuna salad. All of a sudden, my ears tuned in to the radio.

At that point I was a year and a half into intensive therapy and nutritional counseling for anorexia and compulsive over-exercising. My six-year relationship with an amazing man was on the rocks, my friendships were weak, and my family no longer knew the real Me. I realized I needed and wanted to break the destructive cycle of the eating disorder, but kept waiting for that "magic key" to turn. I kept hoping for Santa to bring me health, happiness, and a fudge sundae with no calories. Then, as I was listening to you, I was truly inspired for the first time in my recovery process.

You validated for me the fact that there is something innately and physiologically different inside those with eating disorders, in particular those suffering from anorexia. Finally! I thought. Someone else understands that anorexia is an interwoven chemical and environmental disease—something that can never be obliterated from the personality, but rather that can be worked through and with to create a peaceful life.

Yes, the personality traits that lead to an eating disorder will be with you forever. But each of us has the power to convert those intense characteristics to a more positive nature. Life *can* be lived happily and eating-disorder-free, even though those tendencies may always be lurking.

Everything in my life has bloomed since I took the final plunge into recovery, and didn't turn back as my body came back to life. I cried, I punched pillows, I yelled at therapists and loved ones—and I've never been happier.

I have been at a healthy, stable weight for six months—wow, it takes my breath away to think about that. Each day is still a constant battle between healthy and negative thoughts, realizing my genetic components do not call for size 0 jeans, that a piece of pie will not kill me, and most importantly, realizing it's OK to embrace the imperfections of life! It's my choice what personality traits I want to honor. While I'll always have an eating disorder in my past, it does not need to rule the present or my future.

Kate: Facing the Demons of Dieting

Kate first began suffering from eating disorders at age eight. She's partially recovered and relapsed several times. Only recently, as a young wife and mother, has she finally reached her turning point.

I'VE BEEN AWARE of my problems for many years and have gone through years of feeling recovered. But I always found my way back to my old habits.

I'd done really well for about five years until my wedding loomed, and stress and control took over, and the fear of not fitting into my dress drowned me. I quickly dropped in weight. After the wedding and some help from friends and family, I gained back the weight and moved on. Four years later I gave birth to my son and, though I didn't feel like I had returned to my old ways, I knew I wanted and had to lose the baby weight. I kept telling myself I wasn't anorexic anymore and couldn't be because of my son. But looking back, the habits I used to lose weight were textbook: I *had* to be the skinniest new mom, and I *needed* people to tell me, "Wow, you just had a baby?"

I've always compared my disorder to that of an alcoholic. I'm a diet-holic. Just as recovered alcoholics can't have a drink, I can't diet, take diet pills, or even exercise more than walking. I understand my disorder as if I'm another person analyzing myself. I've studied it: my OCD (obsessive-compulsive disorder), my striving for perfection. It's my oldest "friend." I've known it practically my whole life. It's hard to know how else to be.

My breaking point happened about a month ago when I started counting calories . . . something I promised I'd never do again. I became obsessed, and the day my husband asked if I'd done the laundry, and I hadn't, I started shaking violently and screaming at myself for failing him as a housewife, failing my son. Anxiety had taken over and I was smack in the middle of my demons.

I must dig back to the years of my life where I didn't think about it, where I felt recovered, and find what made me feel complete then. Then I must use the parts of my life that complete me now to create the person I want to be.

Merry: Turning Scared

Merry's story proves it is never too late to recover! She's a wife, mother, and nurse who developed an eating disorder as a child and was hospitalized five times but never fully committed herself to recovering. She was fifty-one when fear finally brought her to her turning point.

BEFORE MY LAST ADMISSION, I was aware that I was dying. I wasn't able to tolerate the low weights as easily as when I was younger. My heart muscles were deteriorating as they were metabolized for energy. My chest pain and shortness of breath felt scary and awful. My kidneys were starting to fail. During my three-week wait to get admitted, my care providers and my family were afraid that I'd have a heart attack in my sleep. I needed IV fluids with electrolytes almost every day at my local clinic. That's when I hit bottom. For the first time I was scared.

I took a different approach in this last admission, trying to be more open to the care of the knowledgeable staff. I made myself more vulnerable. It was not an easy thing to do. I had to let go of some of my willfulness, and to try to face my fears. That was a huge step in finding out who I am. I can feel little crinkles near my eyes and a huge smile spread across my face right now thinking about how much progress I have made.

Stay tuned for more of Merry's story. We'll follow the later phases of her recovery in chapters to come. But her turning point raises the important issue of reading your body's signs and symptoms, recognizing the real damage an eating disorder can do so that you can tell when you physically need treatment. Eating disorders involve both emotional and physical dysregulation that can sometimes be life-threatening. It is critical to know the distress signals that may arise as you move toward physical stabilization and recovery.

DISTRESS SIGNALS
Physical Signs and Symptoms Associated with Eating Disorders
By Nuray O. Kanbur and Debra K. Katzman

Eating disorders can have harmful effects on almost every organ in the body. Some physical signs and medical complications can occur immediately, while others may occur later. Children, adolescents, and adults who suffer from eating disorders should be regularly monitored by health professionals (doctors or nurses) who are familiar with these disorders. These professionals can evaluate the nature and severity of the physical health problem and decide whether to recommend outpatient monitoring or an admission to hospital. Most people who suffer with an eating disorder will do well with appropriate treatment. Outlined below are some of the physical signs and symptoms associated with eating disorders.

SYSTEM	ANOREXIA NERVOSA	BULIMIA NERVOSA	BINGE EATING DISORDER
General	Weight loss Weight loss or lack of weight gain Feeling cold Dehydration Fatigue Irritability/mood changes Depression Low core body temperature	Weight fluctuations Irritability/ mood changes Dehydration Fatigue	Weight gain Fluctuations in weight Overweight or obese Mood changes Depression Anxiety

SYSTEM	ANOREXIA NERVOSA	BULIMIA NERVOSA	BINGE EATING DISORDER
Head, Eyes, Ears, Nose, and Throat	Dry, cracked lips and tongue	Dry lips and tongue Palatal scratches Sore throat Painful teeth and gums Tooth decay or cavities Dental enamel erosion Parotid gland swelling	Gum infections Tooth decay or cavities
Cardiovascular	Dizziness Chest pain Abnormal beating of the heart: too fast, too slow, or irregular heart rate Very slow heart rate, also known as bradycardia Sudden drop in blood pressure when going from a lying or sitting position to a standing position Cold and/or blue hands and feet Poor circulation to hands and feet Ankle swelling Heart failure	Dizziness Chest pain Abnormal beating of the heart: too fast, too slow, or irregular heart rate Sudden drop in blood pressure when going from a lying or sitting position to a standing position Ankle swelling	Shortness of breath Chest pain Stroke High blood pressure

SYSTEM	ANOREXIA NERVOSA	BULIMIA NERVOSA	BINGE EATING DISORDER
Pulmonary		Aspiration (entry of foreign material in lungs), pneumonia	Pauses in breathing during sleep, also called sleep apnea
Gastrointestinal	Feeling full sooner than normal or after eating less than usual Episodes of abdominal pain and discomfort Constipation Bloating after meals	Heartburn Blood in vomitus Mid-upper belly tenderness Diarrhea or constipation Peptic ulcers Pancreatitis	Heartburn Digestive problems Feeling uncomfortably full after eating Gall bladder disease
Metabolic	Chemical/electrolyte (salts in the blood and body fluid) imbalance in the body that affects the heart and other major organ functions	Chemical/electrolyte (salts in the blood and body fluid) imbalance in the body that affects the heart and other major organ functions	High cholesterol
Kidney	Bedwetting Frequent urination Kidney stones		
Endocrine	Absent menses Bone fractures Delay in the onset of pubertal development Growth delay	Absent or irregular menses	Irregularities in blood sugar Type 2 diabetes

SYSTEM	ANOREXIA NERVOSA	BULIMIA NERVOSA	BINGE EATING DISORDER
Dermatologic	Dry skin Pale color to the skin Fine downy hair called lanugo on the cheeks, upper arms, chest, thighs Brittle nails Yellow or orange discoloration of skin, called carotenoderma Thin, dry hair	Calluses on the back of the hand known as Russell's sign Dry mouth	Excessive sweating
Musculoskeletal	Fatigue, muscle weakness, and cramps	Fatigue, muscle weakness, and cramps	Decreased mobility Joint and muscular pain Osteoarthritis
Neurological	Decreased concentration, memory, thinking ability Peripheral nerve damage Structural brain changes	Decreased concentration, memory, thinking ability	Difficulty sleeping and poor sleeping habits Headache

Lynette: Removing the Mask

Lynette, now thirty-seven, had suffered from bulimia for fifteen years when she realized her career was making her sick. She was a TV news anchor. She wrote to me during her first year in recovery, after she'd taken off her mask and stepped away from the camera.

I NEVER HAD EATING PROBLEMS or even thought about dieting or body image in high school or college. However, when I began a career in TV news, I started bingeing and purging. I thought I looked fat on TV. My career was based in large part on my looks. I was never told or instructed to look a certain way, never really felt harassed by management, but I had a big chip on my shoulder. I was damned if I'd let anyone think I was going to skate on my looks. So I went out of my way to prove my worth in the newsroom. I worked my way up as a reporter to the anchor chair. I knew how to shoot and edit my own stories and I'd produce my own newscasts. As I realized I couldn't handle the intense scrutiny of being the "TV lady" and living up to others' expectations, bulimia became my coping mechanism. I lived a double life, completely disconnected from what I really wanted.

As my name and face became better known in the community, I pulled further into myself and away from people. For some reason, it made me very uncomfortable when people would compliment me about how I looked, or say that I was thin ("Look! She can eat whatever she wants and she doesn't gain weight!"). If you're a beautiful woman in society today, your life must be perfect. It was incomprehensible to others that I might have insecurities or my own fears.

I left TV at the height of my career, and a lot of people couldn't understand why. Of course, I know: I'd reached a point where I no longer understood who I was under the public façade.

Now that I've left, I have the space to focus on my issues: perfectionism, trying to find ways to cope with anxiety, thinking someone I love will make me a whole person, feeling that I'm not worth all the good things I've earned.

I believe I have finally laid the groundwork and found the right therapist who will help me manage what seems like a chronic illness. We both realize there are deeper issues at work—that I have to learn healthier ways of coping with my anxieties—to find what makes me happy, as opposed to what others believe will make me happy.

Erin: Completing the Turn

Turning points can occur throughout the process of recovery. Erin had wrestled with anorexia in her adolescence, but considered herself recovered for more than ten years before a seemingly simple question propelled her toward a new phase.

I VOLUNTEER WITH the Massachusetts Eating Disorder Association leading Hope and Recovery groups for those currently battling the disease.
During one session a woman in the audience raised her hand and asked
me how I knew I was recovered. I stumbled a bit, not actually knowing
how or when I knew. Was I fully recovered? I told her that I knew when I
realized I'd stopped thinking about food obsessively and was able to put
my energy toward "normal" behavior. But later when I got home, I kept
thinking about her question. I still struggle daily with perfection issues,
high anxiety, body image distortion, and inability to make decisions. I
started thinking that perhaps, although my weight and eating habits are
normal, my disease had not fully disappeared. Maybe it was a part of my
being, pumping through every vein of my body like blood.

My mother was anorexic at age fifteen, which is the exact age I became
sick. And as I now begin thinking about starting my own family, I want to
do as much work as I can on myself in order to prevent this from happening to my daughter or son. I'm going back into therapy.

Lee: Worth Saving

*Now in her forties, Lee has had an eating disorder for more than
twenty years. She is an associate professor of medicine with four
graduate degrees and three children. She's been through divorce and
remarried. Despite all her accomplishments, she doubted the value of
her life—until she reached her turning point.*

THROUGH MEDICAL SCHOOL I really thought I was cured, but when my
marriage ended at age thirty, I went on "the divorce diet." Though I got
back on track within fifteen months, I buried myself with work, three children, and a busy academic medical career. When my research took off last
year and I started getting national attention within my field, I freaked right
out. My weight had steadily risen, reaching an all-time high. I resorted to
old coping strategies: exercising compulsively and restricting.

Two weeks ago I made the decision that I need to be normal again.
I know exactly when I came to that realization. My therapist was really
worried that I wasn't thinking clearly and might faint because I'd been

fasting. He brought me toast and tea. Not that I could eat it, but it finally dawned on me that someone thought I might actually be worth saving. That, coupled with the warmth of our first really sunny spring day, helped me decide that I want to just be normal and be around to watch my children grow old. I need to do whatever I can to ensure that they avoid this wretched affliction.

I'm hardwired to be anxious, but I recognize now that I can be in control of my interaction with the world. I have to exert myself and stop being passive. But first, I need to figure out who I am and what I want to be.

TWO

Setting the Stage for Recovery

EATING DISORDERS LIE. They deceive us into believing that whatever and however much we eat is wrong. They insist that whatever we weigh is shameful, and that whatever size or shape we may be is never good enough. When it comes to recovery, however, the most pernicious lie in ED's arsenal has nothing directly to do with eating. Rather, it's the notion that we "need" to be left alone.

In fact, it's not the person but the illness that depends on isolation. Starving, bingeing, and purging are secretive and solitary behaviors that feed on shame. And shame itself is alienating. Shame tells us that no one else could possibly understand, care for, or help us. Shame insists that we don't deserve friends or loved ones, especially not those who attempt to nourish us. Shame makes sure that we feel alone in the world, and stranded. As a result, isolation becomes the hollow core around which an eating disorder spirals.

The next step, then, after you've reached your turning point and genuinely committed yourself to recovery, is to confront that lie of isolation. In truth, no one on earth is alone. There are billions of us here! And we're all, to greater and lesser degrees, related by our mutual flaws and yearnings, our weaknesses and frustrations—and by our essential human appetites. Those appetites—for nourishment, love, pleasure, and meaning—deserve to be shared and celebrated, not hidden behind closed doors. When you're trapped in ED's lie, however, it may seem as if everyone else is celebrating and you're not invited to the party. To free yourself, you need to reach out to a few trusted individuals who are willing and able to reintroduce you to your own appetite for life.

Think of this as setting the stage for recovery. You may feel as if you're alone on this stage—alone but for the domineering voice of ED, of course. But actually, crowding in the wings is a large cast of friends, family, teachers, pets, classmates and colleagues, doctors and therapists. Some have known you your whole life; others may have just met you. Some are worried for you, but don't know what to do. Others have the tools to help but need your permission to approach. Many are as baffled and frustrated by ED as you are, and will gladly support you in your battle—if only you'll let them.

You have the power and the right to choose who will join you in the fight for your health, and who won't. Staying out there alone with ED, however, is not a viable option. ED's end goal is to empty that stage of everyone—including you. In other words, ED's finale is death.

Recovery means opting for life. And life demands relationship. To set the stage for recovery, you need to exercise your power to connect with others. If that sounds daunting, it's probably because ED's convinced you of another lie—that you're powerless to make your own choices, especially when it comes to love and trust. Instead of allowing you to relate normally to other people, ED insists that you fixate on your body. The longer you've had an eating disorder, the more difficult it may be to accurately see or hear the people around you. But try to pay closer attention to the individuals who share your daily life. Consider how you're connected and how each one of them makes you feel. How has your illness affected them? How much do they want to help you? What could they contribute to your recovery? What would you need to do to help them help you?

Think of yourself as a casting director. Before a play is cast, actors must audition. The casting director pays close attention to each person's voice, expression, and body language. He considers which of these individuals will be best for the production—who'll bring the most genuine energy, useful skills, and honest commitment to the common effort.

The people you choose to help you set your stage for recovery should meet the same criteria. They'll support you without judging you or tearing you down. They'll make a genuine effort to understand what's wrong, and do their utmost to help you figure out how best to make it right. They'll admit they don't have all the answers, and they'll doubtless have a few flaws of their own. (Not even the healthiest, sanest, most loving people on earth are perfect!) But they *are* wholeheartedly there for you, for your health, for your well-being. You need them, and they need you.

It's worth noting that sometimes the friend who can offer the greatest sense of reassurance and acceptance may not be a human being. In *Gaining* I wrote about the powerful role that horses are playing in some treatment programs, and several readers wrote to me about the importance of animals in their recovery. "She has changed my life," one forty-eight-year-old woman wrote about her Morgan mare. "She's taught me about commitment and selflessness. And for the first time since I was twelve, my eating disorder came in second place. Last night when I went to see her, I thought about how horses reflect our own emotions. As I was thinking that thought, she backed up, turned around, and stared right into my eyes for the longest time."

In most cases, however, the crew that's most eager to set the stage for your recovery will be your family. That's because ED is making them suffer right along with you. As one woman wrote, while her son was held hostage by his eating disorder for four years, through multiple hospitalizations, the whole family had been traumatized. Now, she said, each and every one of them was struggling to define a path for recovery that would bring both her son and the family through intact.

According to Stanford professor Rebecka Peebles, MD (private correspondence), ED makes this struggle particularly challenging for families of younger patients:

> I continue to be impressed by how, for lack of a better word, demonic some kids are when in the early stages of refeeding. They hit, scream, throw things, cut, and wield threatening objects or language to try to avoid eating. They are not at all themselves—sweet and compliant good kids. Consequently, their parents are often truly surprised and fearful of their kids in this phase, and need lots of support to stay firm. ED puts families under siege and disempowers parents profoundly, and many parents don't behave their absolute best when they see their kids wasting away and don't know what to do. If they tend to be on the overprotective or anxious side, their reactions may appear to be very controlling or lacking in boundaries.

However, this truly does improve when they enter into family-based therapy with an experienced clinician.

Even before therapy begins, though, families of patients of all ages can come together by learning the facts about ED. Many parents and partners, out of shame or guilt, mistakenly blame themselves or believe the ED is under their loved one's control. Others, out of frustration or fear, may refuse to believe that their loved one is seriously ill. It can be reassuring for everyone to learn that genetics play a primary role in the development of these illnesses, and that no one actively chooses either to have or to cause an eating disorder.

The metaphor of a gun best describes how eating disorders actually develop. Genes create the gun in the form of certain highly sensitive temperaments that are accompanied by a biological tendency to deal with anxiety through eating behavior. Environmental conditions and attitudes, such as cultural and family values that emphasize looks and status over substance, load the gun. And emotional distress, which may range from intense trauma or abuse to adolescent anxiety over identity and independence, pulls the trigger.

What all this means is that eating disorders actually serve a function: they fire a warning shot to signal that something emotionally profound is amiss. However, this function is only useful if the person affected and those around her learn to read and respond appropriately to the signal. If the gun is not disarmed, the signaling can turn lethal.

Reading the signals is difficult in a society that holds up emaciated actors and models as standards of beauty. It's also difficult in families that consider it healthy to be unnaturally thin or compulsively fit and busy. Parents, siblings, partners, and friends who have never questioned their own pursuit of idealized looks can easily fail to connect the dots when a person they love becomes dangerously obsessed with her or his weight. Sadly, the push to achieve and look good to the outside world can override honest communication.

But the emphasis on appearance is not the only obstacle. When I began interviewing other people with histories of eating disorders, I realized that almost all of us had relatives with eating disorders. Yet often the illness was denied, self-starvation even defended as "discipline" within the family. In some families, everyone was so respectful of each other's need for "space" that intimacy and trust collapsed. In others, honesty was met with violence or rejection. Then, when everyday pressures were compounded, whether by something as mundane as a verbal insult or as serious as a death in the family, the person who never raised her voice, much less misbehaved, turned her imperfect pain against herself.

The letters in this chapter show that recovery represents a critical opportunity for everyone in the family to cut through the isolation, shed the shame, and disarm the gun. The person who's "sick" is never truly alone. Whether the rest of the family consists of parents or siblings, a concerned spouse and children, close friends or a beloved animal, everyone has a stake in recovery, and every member who's able and willing has an important role to play.

Zahara: A Family Affair

When Zahara wrote me, I was struck by the sorrow and confusion this bright Egyptian-English woman still feels at age twenty-six, having battled various aspects of anorexia since she was thirteen. Although she's now maintaining a healthy weight, her letter makes clear that many of the contributing factors—which include some fascinating cultural elements—remain unresolved. Even though she and her sister both struggle with eating disorders, her family has been unable thus far to come together and set the stage for their recovery.

THE MOST INFURIATING QUESTION during the time I was unwell was "why?"

My mother is British, my father Egyptian. My sister and I were born in London and brought up there until I was seven years old. However, we had a home in Egypt too, where we spent about six months of the year. A massive part of the Egyptian culture is food. Food was the center of every social gathering and, until my anorexia started, I always enjoyed this activity with my Egyptian family.

My dad and other family members used food to express their love. Food can solve all problems, or at least it is a distraction. And being a bigger size, especially for a woman, is the beauty ideal in Egypt. Curvy women are envied, slim women are ridiculed. I was always slim and active. My sister, on the other hand, was always rather overweight. They loved her for this and always tried to force-feed me more and teased me for being so skinny.

Interestingly, my sister developed Binge Eating Disorder, although the family always believed she just had a big appetite, which was celebrated in our Egyptian culture. I was the abnormal one, not her. Years later she developed bulimia. She's never wanted to seek help and never talks about either disorder.

After fourteen years of marriage, things started to go badly for my parents. Mum decided to move me and my sister to the rural area up in northern England where my three older half sisters from Mum's previous marriage lived. I was the baby of five daughters. Then Mum and Dad decided to give their marriage one last shot with a holiday in Egypt. This is where the nightmare really began. I was eight years old.

After a month in Egypt, Mum said it was time to return home with me and my sister for the new school term. Dad turned nasty and said the only way Mum would be leaving the country was in a box, and my sister and I would never leave. Of course, I never knew any of this until years later. My mum turned to my ten-year-old sister for support. I thought we were having a lovely time—until I was grabbed from my bed in the early hours of the morning by my mum, sister by my side, and we drove to the British Embassy.

We had to take a bus to Israel and forge Mum's passport to include me and my sister, as Dad wouldn't give her our passports back. Dad didn't know we were back in England until a month later.

I lived in England then with my mother and sister, not returning to Egypt for holidays until I was sixteen years old. Dad moved to London so that he could come visit us.

Part of the Egyptian culture is to not talk about how you are feeling. Crying is very much a hysterical act and should be avoided at all costs. When Dad used to bring us home after a trip out with him, my sister would be overcome with emotions, crying and screaming about not wanting him to leave. I could see the pain on my parents' faces from her outbursts; my mum would comfort her for hours after each visit. I'd just stand there numb, wave dutifully, go upstairs in my room, and cry for hours alone.

Nobody ever asked how I felt. They assumed I was coping just fine because I was always so together and calm. Plus I was an A student, whereas my sister was always doing badly and getting into trouble at school. It was obvious that my sister had suffered the worst from the divorce. If only they'd realized . . .

When I started high school I was twelve years old. I felt odd, uncomfortable with my name, especially when new teachers would mispronounce it and the other kids would laugh. I felt that when I spoke or played or went out with friends I was putting on a show, and that if they found out who the real me was, they would laugh in my face.

Things took a bad turn when I became close to a girl I envied. She was everything I wanted to be. Blond hair, blue eyes, gorgeous. I was always comparing myself to her, and always feeling fat and ugly, whereas I've always been skinny really. When we found her mum's Cher workout video, we did it for a laugh. My mum thought it was good I was doing some exercise and so was happy to buy me a copy. Soon I was working out alone, sometimes two or three times a day. At the same time, I started to eat "healthily." I suddenly developed a dairy allergy and cut out lots of food groups that began to make me feel sick. Since I was already skinny before this started, it didn't take long for my weight to plummet.

Not one person in my family noticed the trouble I was in until the GP (General Practice physician) confirmed it. I remember my mother throwing a plate of food at me after I refused to eat; she was so full of rage for what I was doing to her. She thought I could stop my "self-indulgence" if I wanted to.

It broke my dad's heart. Eating used to be what we enjoyed doing together the most—sitting on the hood of his car munching our way through a family bucket of KFC, or him teaching me how to cook Egyptian cuisine. If he couldn't feed me, he didn't know how to make it better. In Egypt, if you're slim, the parents are blamed for not feeding you well, or are accused of not having enough wealth to provide for your family. My anorexia was like spitting in his face, stomping all over the things he believed in. He just shouted at me.

I'm pretty sure my parents both believed I was doing it to punish them. And yet British culture was giving me a totally opposite message. At school everyone brought in packed lunches, the contents of which were very specific: no mayonnaise or butter in sandwiches and no chocolate, or it would make you fat!

I've always thought that Dad finally saying to me that he didn't want me to die helped me decide to recover, but there are many reasons why I developed anorexia. I felt nobody understood me or tried to. I was reaching out, wanting my parents to unite and help me instead of always fighting. Girls at school were always talking about their weight and what new diet they were on. I copied my new school friends because I wanted to fit in, to be liked. I was so scared of being alone at school; I was alone enough at home.

I now see that not being able to connect with my parents, not being able to stand up to them, regressing into a child when with them—all these are entangled with my eating disorder. Neither of my parents nor my sisters nor my Egyptian family discuss my anorexia. It's almost like a terrible family secret that must not be discussed.

Pam: Breaking Away

> When Pam wrote me, she was twenty-two years old and had struggled with eating disorders for sixteen hard years. After being adopted, then molested by a family member at an early age, she lost her father when she was ten. The already active fault lines within her family widened as lawsuits over her father's company and estate pitted her mother and Pam against her four older brothers. Meanwhile, eating disorders had a strong history in this family. Pam's mother channeled her stress through food restriction, as well as substance abuse, and her grandmother had died of her eating disorder. Although Pam was not genetically related to the disease, she associated eating disorders and other self-destructive behavior with her love for her mother. To set the stage for her recovery, she needed to discover—and believe— that healthier sources of love were available to her.

I REMEMBER MY MOTHER teaching me to purge my food when I was in first grade. I was put into mandatory counseling then, but I didn't understand anything was wrong with me. My life revolved around food and weight, idolizing my mother and all she did. My eating disorder was my bond with her. When I was older, we would always smoke together, drink together, go to shows together. I was her date. She beat me, verbally abused me, used drugs with me. I lied about every bruise, even when she broke my ribs.

When I was sixteen, I had a gynecology appointment because I'd lost my period. My eyes were bloodshot, my cheeks puffy little chipmunk cheeks, and my glands were swollen. The gynecologist noticed this but left it alone, until she asked when my last period was. I replied, "Over a year ago."

"How long have you had an eating disorder?"

I broke down crying. I hadn't let anyone hug me in years, but that sweet doctor took me in her arms and held me while I cried.

Then she told my mother, who laughed and wouldn't sign the intake papers. I went out and overdosed, which got me almost a month in the psych ward. There they finally listened to me and brought me to the Eating Disorders Unit (EDU).

My mother was forbidden to visit me because she would let me smoke and run around when I was supposed to be in the wheelchair. She came banging on the glass doors of the EDU, drunk and screaming for me to come home. I wanted to go to her because she was hurting. I wanted to save her, but at the same time I knew what happened when she was drunk, and it was so safe in the EDU. No one would hurt me there but myself. I stood there until they escorted her away.

They said I had the emotional comprehension of a five-year-old. In the EDU I was to spend days doing little-kid stuff like playing and coloring, watching kid movies, listening to stories at bedtime. . . . I totally embraced this and let myself fall back into my childlike state. I believe it was the most healing thing I've ever done. I think it was how I grew up. . . . I learned to make friends, and I learned that the power was all mine. I had a voice . . . a voice I'd locked away for sixteen years.

WHAT'S ED HIDING?
Setting the Stage for Recovery from an Eating Disorder Rooted in Trauma

By Yael Latzer

Eating disorders sometimes begin as a reaction to trauma. The loss of a loved one, physical or emotional abuse, divorce in the family, an unexpected relocation or job loss—these are just a few of the traumatic events that can trigger feelings of shame, insecurity, fear, and helplessness, which ED serves to muffle or numb. Paradoxically, while self-starvation, excessive bingeing, and purging are self-destructive behaviors, the subjective intentions that drive them are often self-*protective*. ED's rules, regulations, and rituals can create a false sense of security, control, and predictability to a life shattered by trauma. They also give the illusion of purpose to a life that otherwise may feel meaningless.

If you're recovering from an eating disorder that's rooted in trauma, your turning point may come as soon as you recognize this linkage. Life before this experience might seem in retrospect like your "perfect" life; after the trauma you may have felt stranded in a shattered world, unable to find a single person you could trust to share your pain. You may have felt rage, fear, shame, confusion, and detachment. Perhaps your school performance, work, relationships, or even your faith deteriorated. If family and friends expressed disappointment in you, this likely deepened your feeling of isolation. Maybe ED seemed to help you regain a sense of control and relief by overwhelming your pain with the feeling of fullness or purging, or perhaps by dieting and losing weight you gradually became addicted to the sensation of emptiness. These practices may have offered you a way to bear the pain by stifling your true emotional needs, or by making you feel as if you were hiding or disappearing. But it's essential to recognize that ED ultimately will only compound and add new pain. Recovery has to address both the ED symptoms and the underlying experiences that prompted them.

Of course, that kind of exploration can feel very threatening to a trauma survivor. So as you begin to set the stage for your recovery, *safety* is key. The prospect of treatment and change will seem more promising if you seek out safe people, places, and things that help you feel comforted and protected during the process:

Who are your safe people?

Your safe people will not hurt you. They won't disparage you, bully you, or behave in ways that undermine or destroy your growing feelings of self-confidence. A relationship with a trusted therapist or caring friend, family member, or partner can replace ED as a source of security and meaning. A secure relationship can help you feel accepted and appreciated for who you are and provide the secure foundation for all the "next steps" in the recovery process. And if human relationships still seem too daunting, know that safe relationships can also encompass loving pets. Animals can provide warm, unconditional love and be highly sensitive companions.

Where are your safe places?

Your safe place is a location where you feel grounded and "like yourself"—even after a difficult day or stretch in recovery. This place should be familiar, predictable, and easy to reach. Yours may be your bedroom, your house or apartment (or a small area within your house or apartment), a favorite park, place of worship, or even a well-lit coffee shop bustling with people and comforting smells. It's important to have as many safe places as possible that you can return to, either physically or in your mind, as you work through the effects of trauma.

What are your safe things?

Safe things are our adult security blankets. These soothing and un-failing sources of comfort might include a pair of comfortable paja-mas; an old, cozy sweater; a cup of your favorite tea; a CD or movie DVD that always makes you feel better; a favorite poem or piece of music. Your safe things consistently make you feel a bit better. Make sure you always have at least one readily at hand.

In addition to seeking specialized care for your eating disorder and trauma experience don't hesitate to turn to your safe people, places, and things for support and comfort. Each time you do, your attachment to ED as your coping mechanism will lessen. Your sense of confidence in yourself and your feelings of safety in the world around you will grow. These will give you the foundation you need to move forward in recovery.

Lauren and Gillian: Keep No Secrets

Lauren and her daughter, Gillian's, letters tell a dramatically different story than Pam's and Zahara's. Thanks in part to Lauren's experience as a learning specialist and former dean of a girls' school, she was familiar with the warning signs of eating disorders. But Gillian was only about seven when she began to develop anorexia, and Lauren didn't know how to read the signals of such an early onset. Gillian was fourteen by the time Lauren stepped in to help her daughter. Unfortunately, by then Gillian was firmly in ED's grip. But Lauren and her husband hung in there, and now Gillian is eighteen, attends college in her hometown, and is thinking of majoring in psychology and communications. She hopes someday to work for a treatment center. Although mother and daughter both recognize that the ultimate responsibility for recovery is Gillian's, their reflections make clear that every member of this family has played a role in helping her get well.

Lauren, Gillian's Mother

IT'S VERY EASY to ignore a problem. You can rationalize that it's really no big deal. You can wait and see if it goes away. You can try to solve it on your own, or you can decide to confront it. Confronting anorexia has been the most difficult thing we've ever done.

I can understand why so many parents, friends, and spouses ignore it, hoping it will go away on its own. To acknowledge it, to say out loud that it's really there, means you now must deal with it. Dealing with it as a parent is lifelong. Sure, it won't always be as painful or difficult as it is in the beginning, but it will always be there, just under the surface waiting to rear its ugly head and turn your life and the lives of everyone in the family upside down.

I have to admit, although I was never afraid of confronting my daughter about her eating disorder, I had no idea how much our lives would change. I figured that I'd talk to her; we'd go to her doctor, see a therapist, and after a bit of time, several months, perhaps, the anorexia would go away. She'd still play lacrosse that spring, we'd go on our annual family vacation, and she'd go to summer camp as planned.

My husband was out of town on business, and he felt I was imagining things or overreacting. I told him over the phone that I thought our daughter had anorexia and I was going to talk to her. He wanted to be there too, but I didn't want to wait any longer. I'd been watching her for a few weeks. She'd been taking her lunch to school: snack-size bag of cereal and Propel (an energy drink). Sometimes, all of the cereal wasn't gone, so I'd have her eat it at home. Her sweatpants were baggy, and she was very careful and deliberate about her dinner. My previous job, dean of an all-girls' middle school, had allowed me to talk to a number of girls with eating disorders, and I'd been reading and researching anorexia. I had found too many similarities.

She'd just gotten out of the shower, and I asked her to come to the kitchen to talk. She rolled her eyes, like teenagers do when you want to discuss something important. I sat at the table. She stood, arms crossed. I told her I knew something was going on. Although I knew what it was, I didn't want to say it initially; I wanted to give the conversation a chance to get going, in hopes that she might admit it on her own. I finally said, "I think you have an eating disorder." She became very defensive and told me I had no idea what I was talking about.

Up until now, no voices had been raised. I told her about the dangers of anorexia, both short-term and long-term. She told me I was crazy. I told her maybe I didn't know because I wasn't a doctor, but her pediatrician would know, and we'd be seeing her the day after next.

First thing next morning, I called her pediatrician. I filled her in on everything: behaviors, conversations, and deep concerns. I told her she needed to find something so that we could move on this immediately.

The day of her appointment, her pediatrician came in and asked to speak with her alone. After about twenty minutes, I joined in on the conversation. The doctor said that she had the beginning stages of an eating disorder. Her weight was down; her personality was flat; her body temperature was lower than normal and she was cold; and she was overly concerned about calories. She needed to come in once a week to get weighed, and she needed to begin to see a nutritionist and therapist. Little conversation took place on the way home. I told her I loved her and would be there to help.

For the next three weeks, our schedule was the same: pediatrician weigh-in, nutritionist meal plans, and therapy sessions. After their first meeting, the therapist was able to tell that my daughter's mind-set was so strong, she would probably need a partial hospitalization program. My daughter was in complete denial, and she barely spoke a word during the sessions. We all discussed the possibility of residential treatment, but it never seemed like a reality to her. That is, until week number three.

After that week's therapy appointment, I called the treatment program and left a message stating that we needed to get an evaluation. I hadn't heard back by the following day, so I called again. Fortunately, we were able to get an appointment in two weeks. Forms would be sent, and insurance information submitted. The process had begun.

When you're faced with a crisis, you need to learn everything you can about that crisis from everyone and anyone who will offer their advice or personal stories. At first, there's no sifting through information. You just hang on to every word in the hope that there will be a magical panacea. For us, being part of a family support group was our initiation.

Our first family meeting was on the Monday evening after our daughter had been admitted to PHP (partial hospitalization program). In a large, cold, impersonal room, parents gathered to talk. We entered, selected three seats (our nine-year-old son was with us), and we all looked like deer in a headlight. Names were exchanged, and then the stories began. Parents told us not to worry, that soon we'd see progress. Our daughter needed to be nourished. Her brain was being starved and all of her food was going to keep her heart beating. They'd been there. We wouldn't believe how much better she'd be after even a week in the program. I wept and prayed as our son listened, hoping his sister wouldn't die. Parents offered advice on how to be strong, take time for yourself, and accept the fact that your life will never be the same. You'll never look at your child the same way you did before the eating disorder. You'll never have the same life you had before the eating disorder. You're all different now. Accept that.

Because we were at an eating-disorder program that followed the family-based treatment approach known as the Maudsley method, parents shared stories of the countless ways that they passed time while waiting for their child to complete a meal. We could play games (the ABC game and Twenty Questions became our favorites), talk about vacations, read (*Ripley's Believe It or Not* got us through many a meal), or even color to make the minutes go more quickly. We needed to realize that meals were no longer pleasurable. They dragged on and on. They were a test of wills, ours and ED's.

As I absorbed every minute detail, I realized that this group of strangers was going to be my sanity, my library, my lifeline to normalcy. I didn't know any of them and had little in common with them before I entered that room. Now, they'd be closer to me and know more about my pain and suffering than even my own family. They would assure me I wasn't going crazy and that things would get better.

After that first family group, I continued to read about anorexia in books, magazines, and journals. I read personal stories from the children themselves; I read stories that parents, journalists, and friends had written. I was still hoping to find something that would wake my daughter up and make her want to get better.

My daughter also read. I gave her articles and had her watch interviews, all in hopes that she'd identify with something or someone, that something I could get my hands on would work.

Our journey with anorexia officially began over three and a half years ago, but for our daughter, it is still a work in progress. Thanks to continuing individual, family, and group therapy coupled with in-patient, residential, day, and outpatient treatment, she's recovering from her eating disorder. Not a meal goes by that I'm not thankful for where we are, not a moment goes by that normalcy is not celebrated. I cannot be thankful enough for mundane dinner conversations or for watching a movie, eating popcorn and M&Ms. I am truly grateful for every new day. I always told my daughter that everything happens for a reason, and I've always believed this. We were meant to tell our story and help others.

Gillian

I WAS ALWAYS SEEN as small and a picky eater, but because my eating disorder began at such a young age, none of these primary symptoms were regarded with concern. I lived for eight years with a silent and unknown, yet overpoweringly strong eating disorder, which made seemingly insignificant health problems, such as intestinal issues and lack of energy, a part of my everyday life.

I never hid my eating disorder from friends or family. This has ultimately given me an unimaginable amount of support and understanding.

I've let my friends help me in any way they can, though sadly I've had to learn that those who cannot support me are not friends I can have at this time. Although this has led to me losing a few good friends, I've also realized who I can count on to always be there for me. My openness with friends and family has led to the strength to speak out about the truth and horrors of eating disorders, and I've found public speaking to be extremely empowering.

Finding a therapist with whom I clicked proved to be priceless. Although it took around two years to find the right therapist for me, I tell anyone who's beginning the journey of recovery that they must not settle for anything other than the best. It must feel comfortable and even sometimes fun talking with your therapist, because that makes the hard times surmountable. You must not lose hope when looking for the right person. Think of that as part of your recovery, because you *cannot* do it alone.

The third crucial part of my recovery may be slightly controversial, though I feel I would be remiss not to tell the full story. The concoction of medications that I'm taking at the moment has proved as vital as any other part of my treatment. I know many patients are reluctant to take meds due to the possible side effect of weight gain. This was a huge fear of mine, but my psychiatrist, who I trust deeply, explained to me that the meds simply increase appetite, and I personally was not at all worried about having an increased appetite. So after three years of trying multiple medications and learning the hard way how certain ones were affecting me, I've found the medication that's gotten me to this place of contentment.

Group therapy was very helpful to me, though I know that groups may worry some parents of younger patients. There can be some fear that younger kids in a group may actually pick up new habits from older kids. And although I won't deny that's possible, being around other people who are struggling is a way to get a sort of support that can't be gained any other way. So I urge families to address this worry with a therapist if need be, but seriously consider how alone your child most likely feels with this disease.

Lastly, spirituality has played a large part in my recovery. As I've started to gain clarity and sanity, the strong belief that I'm not struggling and living alone and that I have a purpose and won't change who I am by altering my appearance has helped me more willingly accept life and recovery.

I see myself as recovering, which I've learned to be content with for as long as need be. Personally, I think time is the only thing that can heal the wounds of this disease. I've accepted that it's best not to rush recovery, to enjoy the successes and be braced for the relapses, and I pray for the same patience for everyone else who is struggling.

THE MAUDSLEY METHOD
How Parents Can Help Their Children and Adolescents
By Angela Celio Doyle

Most of the symptoms experienced by people with anorexia nervosa, from dizziness and feeling cold to irritability and depressed mood, are a result of physical starvation. Likewise, many of the distorted thoughts about food and body weight and shape are reinforced and perpetuated by a low weight. So weight restoration is critical as the first step to recovery. The Maudsley approach empowers parents to help their child, rather than watch passively from the sidelines.

Anorexia nervosa causes true fear of the effects of food and weight gain, so the treatment involves compassionate yet persistent and firm expectations that your child eat an amount of food that can reverse the physical state of starvation. Some families encounter a moderate amount of resistance from their teen during meals, and some encounter a lot. Professionals trained in the Maudsley approach will help parents determine the best way to address the resistance and make three meals and three snacks per day compassionate and successful.

The Maudsley approach is not punitive in any way and involves quite a bit of emotional support. Some parents may fear that they're being insensitive if they push their child to eat a plate of fettuccini Alfredo when the child is refusing, crying, or otherwise resisting. However, if you consider a child with a chronic illness, such as cancer, who pleads with their parent to avoid another bout of chemotherapy because it makes them feel sick, a parent would compassionately yet firmly determine that the chemotherapy is needed, despite how it makes them feel. In this way, some parents of adolescents with anorexia find it helpful to view food as medicine that's required in order to save their child's life, quite literally. It's also important to remember that the resistance to eating stems from the anorexia, not from the healthy, wonderful child who was overtaken by this illness.

Some parents also become concerned that this will harm their relationship with their child. For instance, one father I worked with didn't want to insist on whole milk with every meal because his daughter would cry and sob, saying that it was disgusting. She'd tell him how much she hated him for making her eat calorie-laden meals and snacks. While this was a challenging situation to deal with, when his daughter's weight was fully restored and we'd progressed through the other phases of therapy (that is, handing food control back to the adolescent and facilitating healthy adolescent development), their relationship was positive and strong. The daughter, when finally healthy, could see that her father had done these things because of his love for her and his devotion to keeping her alive.

My clinical experiences are supported by research: in a study by Robin, Siegel, and Moye (1995), parent-adolescent relationships were actually improved after treatment. The take-home message is that although you may face difficult conflicts during treatment due to the anorexia, as the anorexia retreats, conflicts will ultimately subside.

The Maudsley approach also asks siblings, if there are any, to provide emotional support to their sister or brother. The siblings are not involved in the decisions about food or in monitoring eating—that's up to the parents. Instead, a sibling can be someone to complain to, a shoulder to cry on, or a distraction from the difficult task of eating. The exact role will depend on the age and preexisting relationships, but siblings can be incredible resources for helping a teen in recovery.

Once an adolescent is weight-restored and the parents feel confident in their ability to prevent their child from losing weight, decisions about food and eating are slowly and carefully returned to the teen. This is done slowly in order to ensure that the teen is capable of making these decisions without the anorexia making the decisions for her.

Finally, the last phase of the Maudsley approach is focused on establishing a healthy parent-child relationship *that does not involve the anorexia* and restoring normal adolescent development. For instance, some teens with anorexia may become very withdrawn from friends, so one focus might be to improve peer relationships by encouraging age-appropriate activities. The goal is to get these teens back on track with their health, their relationships, and their personal life goals.

*(Excerpted and adapted, with permission, from
http://maudsleyparents.org/maudsleymisconceptions.html.)*

Barbara: Facing the Great Divide

Barbara wrote shortly after discovering that her college-age daughter was bingeing and purging, not only on food but also on alcohol. Her own sense of helplessness seemed to be equaled by her daughter's, yet they were growing increasingly apart. Like so many parents in similar situations, she was terrified for her daughter and desperate for advice.

My daughter is in her last semester of college and has always been an overachiever. We never had to tell her to do her homework or even help her with it because she excelled in school. She's always been fiercely independent. However, she has never seemed truly happy.

After her sophomore year in college, she did a summer internship at a newspaper, in another part of our state, so we didn't see her until August. She'd e-mail me and complain about feeling bloated and having PMS, erratic periods, and mood swings. When we picked her up in August, it was clear that she'd lost a lot of weight and I immediately began to worry. She'd also become a vegetarian and she attributed the weight loss to that and to her work schedule. She still looked healthy, but it was a shock to us.

Now she's facing graduation and job searching. I recently caught her bingeing and purging over her Christmas vacation. She'd also been drinking, and she broke down and told me what she was feeling.

She wants so desperately to be perfect and recognized. This part is so hard for me to grasp because we've always praised her for her successes and she was recognized in school and college with many awards. She has a wonderful boyfriend who adores her. It's rather ironic that she's become a very good cook even though she clearly denies herself food.

The most recent event was the most troubling and terrifying for us. We were away visiting her brother and we received a phone call in the middle of the night from a hospital telling us that she was in the ER with alcohol poisoning and was basically unresponsive but breathing. She'd been celebrating her roommate's birthday at a bar. Her blood alcohol level was almost seven times the legal limit. She was dehydrated and hypothermic as well.

After a long sleepless night, she was released. We let her know that we love her, but we also lectured her (another guilt trip) about the consequences of her actions. (Her father has a history of drinking and bingeing, but stopped himself many years ago.) I even threatened to stop paying the last few months of her tuition unless she gets help. I feel like that's our only leverage in this situation, since she is an adult.

What can we as parents, who love her, do? We can't sit back and watch our daughter possibly kill herself. She has so much to offer this world.

WHAT TO SUGGEST AND HOW TO SUGGEST IT
Talking Tips for Parents to Open Communication
By Janet Treasure and Pam Macdonald

Eating disorders, in particular anorexia nervosa, are linked to driven, perfectionist traits. Often, these perfectionist traits appear to be associated with an eye for detail, which can be a wonderful source of skill and talent when used wisely. Unfortunately, if this trait is applied to the rules and regulations of dieting, it can give the individual a dangerously powerful sense of mastery while depriving her body and brain of nutrition. A vicious circle then begins as rational thought and the capacity to healthfully regulate food intake become diminished.

When one or both parents also possess the traits of perfectionism and drivenness, they may have difficulty providing the emotional support the child needs to help him or her recover. The eye for detail, for example, may lead parents to strive to provide the perfect advice and setting for the child's recovery, placing extraordinary pressure on themselves and the child in the process. Such high expectations can result in what we have termed "rhinoceros behaviors"—the parent uses overly forceful arguments or ultimatums to encourage change. Unfortunately, when the child is not ready or able to hear advice, it can fall on deaf ears or, worse, incite rebellion.

The desire to provide perfect parenting may also lead to what we call "kangaroo behavior"—the parent attempts to take over for their child, to tuck her or him safely out of harm's way (as if into a secure pouch) while the parent takes complete control of the situation. The kangaroo approach overprotects and infantilizes the individual, depriving her of essential opportunities to learn how to meet daily challenges.

The rhinoceros- and kangaroo-parenting responses frequently increase anxiety, both in the individual with the eating disorder and in the parents themselves. And anxiety is contagious, so tensions rapidly escalate, further impeding recovery.

What can parents do to step outside of this frenetic dance and help, rather than hinder, recovery? We recommend "dolphin-style parenting":

- Offer flexible, calm support. Consistent encouragement helps both parent and child keep their focus on the eating disorder and recovery, rather than on relationship struggles and misunderstandings.
- Gently and consistently encourage the child to express the reasons she wants to change and why she is ambivalent about changing. This ambivalence about changing in recovery is common. The eating-disorder rules and regulations are fueled by fear. The individual in recovery must confront this fear with every step forward. Simply providing the safety and room for her to express her ambivalence and to think out loud about the challenges she's facing will help reduce her anxiety and emotional isolation.
- Talk with her about what steps she feels she might be ready to take. Any step, no matter how small, if completed successfully,

can build self-confidence and the strength to take the next step. Recovery comes from taking many small steps.

- Focus on her concerns rather than on the logical reasons why she should recover. The eating-disorder thought process is not rational. Trust, encouragement, and acknowledgment of the difficulties of recovery are more effective than logic.

- Listen, listen, listen to her concerns, then paraphrase what you heard her say to be sure you understand. Knowing she is understood and being listened to will help create a feeling of safety and support that your child can use to face her fears about taking the next steps in her recovery.

It's not easy to practice these behaviors, particularly in the face of life-threatening illness. At the Maudsley Hospital (www.maudsleypar ents.org) we've been developing ways of working in collaboration with parents to provide skills-based training programs that reduce the levels of anxiety and stress in the whole family. The feedback we've received from eating-disorders sufferers suggests that they value the compassion, listening skills, and increased understanding generated by parent training. Parents can be a powerful resource for change.

Lisa and Sheila: Separate Voices

When I received Lisa and her mother, Sheila's, letters, I was reminded that ED can be entangled in the child's struggle to find and articulate her own voice, not only separate from her parents but also, at times, in conflict with them. (Many of us become writers in order to find and hear this voice ourselves.) Sheila and her college-age daughter Lisa chose to tackle this particular element of ED head on when they wrote an article for Sheila's paper about fighting ED as a family. The huge response to the article motivated them to expand it into a book in their two separate voices. Sheila, a food critic and journalist, had made a profession out of writing about her own experience and relationship with food. But it was a new challenge for Lisa, complicated by the fact that she'd only begun to recover. The project ended up taking six years, during which they both learned how to honestly voice

and accept their disagreements. Their finished memoir is entitled,
Hungry: A Mother and Daughter Fight Anorexia. *It stands as a*
testament to the need for all parents and children, but especially
those struggling with eating disorders, to respect, understand, and
listen to each other.

Lisa

Mom and I began to write the newspaper article that would become
our book when I was a freshman at the University of California, Santa
Cruz. I seemed well to the world, getting over my anorexia, but secretly I
was battling extreme bulimia. Our unique situation of my mom as a food
writer with an anorexic/bulimic daughter made for a great and interesting
story, which the San Jose *Mercury News,* where Mom was the restaurant
critic, ran on the front page in December 2003. We received such tremendous, encouraging feedback that it seemed only natural to write a book.

The writing process, however, took us on a long, complicated, and
often painful journey. In the end, our relationship as mother and daughter
grew tremendously. Of course, like any parent and child we still have our
differences and arguments, but writing a book together helped us both
gain a better understanding of each other. Not that there weren't times
when we didn't speak!

I managed to get better for most of my senior year of college, but I
had no professional support system. Instead, I tried to rely on willpower
alone. I just wanted to be able to claim recovery—and have it be easy—but
I set myself up for a tremendous fall. I'd feel great and think my eating
disorders were behind me and then, suddenly, relapse. I might get set off
by some event, maybe school stress got to me or a fight with a boyfriend,
and then I'd find myself back in the bathroom, purging.

The nutritionist I used to see weekly during high school had told me
not to declare myself recovered until I'd been better at least three to five
years. At the time I thought this to be extreme and maybe a little grim. I
figured the day I decided to recover, I was off the hook. Six years later,
after many relapses, and hospitalization in 2007, I realized why she'd said
this. Eating disorders do not run a specific course and neither does recovery. An eating disorder, like any addiction, does not just go away when
one decides to get better. Recovery is a lifelong process that takes hard

work and determination. It's important to seek out a team of specialists and stay connected.

Sheila

THERE WERE TIMES during the writing of our book when Lisa and I fought each other more than we fought the disease. Neither of us would recommend a mother-daughter book project as the road to recovery, but it was the road open to us.

The book went on the back burner more than once. When Lisa had a horrible relapse, our editor, who has children of her own, was very understanding. She didn't pressure me. Our original happy ending had evaporated, but she was convinced that when we could get back to it, a less tidy book would resonate with readers.

Our newspaper article had gotten an overwhelming and heartbreaking response. Readers were incredibly grateful to know that they weren't alone, that other families had been affected by ED and had the same difficulties digging out. Expanding our story for the book would be another opportunity to fight the shame and loneliness that make everything harder for patients, parents, siblings, friends, colleagues, doctors, and therapists who deal with ED.

Lisa and I still have our disagreements about eating disorders, what happened to us, what anyone could have done. But we've learned that by airing our differences, they've lost their power to derail us.

As mother-daughter bonding activities go, writing a book together is formidable even without a life-threatening illness. But it feels great that we did what we set out to do: comfort people who are struggling with this illness, and provide some practical help. *At last,* I can say, "What a great idea!"

Leigha and Brad: Loving Partners

If you are married or involved in a committed relationship, when you have an eating disorder your partner may be even more deeply affected than your parents. What's at stake in every marriage or close relationship is intimacy. But ED preempts intimacy, insisting that the body is a source of shame and secrecy, not pleasure and connec-

*tion. ED also damages relationships by promoting mistrust of any-
one who nurtures normal healthy appetites. How can love possibly
compete? As Leigha and Brad's powerful "duet" letter shows, when
both partners come together on the recovery stage, love not only can
compete, love can triumph.*

Leigha

MY TEN-YEAR STRUGGLE with anorexia and bulimia began as a result of
my parents' divorce. Feeling as though I'd lost all control in my life, I
turned to the only thing I could control: food.

While I was able to cope with my eating disorder for the first several years on my own, once I got married, this battle was no longer just
between me and food; it now involved another party.

Prior to getting married, my husband and I were living in different
states. The only time we really were able to see each other was the occasional weekend. Within such a limited time frame, my husband didn't
truly understand how engrossed I was in the eating disorder. It was not
that I hid it from him, but our focus was on enjoying the limited time
we had together. Once we were married and had moved in together, the
eating-disorder behaviors quickly became evident to him. It was hard for
him to understand why I counted calories and had "safe foods," why I
weighed myself every day and based my daily happiness upon the number
that appeared on the scale, why I took so long to get ready when we went
out, and why I worried so much about what others thought of me. I never
realized how much of my time the eating disorder was taking up on a daily
basis. And my husband was beginning to feel that he was no longer the
important one in the relationship, that food was receiving all the attention. There just wasn't enough room for the three of us.

At this point I knew it was time for a change. This was not something
I could face alone any longer.

Brad

I WAS AWARE that there was an issue while we were dating, but I thought
of it as a minor inconvenience in an otherwise perfect relationship, and a
quirk of sorts in an otherwise wonderful person. I myself am not perfect

and I had no illusion that my soon-to-be wife would be either. However, there are acceptable idiosyncrasies in people, and then there are unhealthy and unacceptable traits that must be addressed.

Only after we were married did I realize the gravity of the entire situation. The eating disorder prevented my wife from obtaining the proper nutrients, from being herself in public, and from experiencing the spontaneous things in life that make it worth living. For our relationship to continue successfully, events could not be perfectly preplanned. Menu choices couldn't always be preselected. She'd need to be able to eat in public. She was going to have to learn how to live life and deal with situations as they occurred, and trust her body's ability to regulate weight naturally.

Leigha

THERAPY WAS MY SAVING GRACE. However, it took quite a bit of patience and diligence on both my husband's part and mine to see the eating disorder from both sides. While I knew this recovery process was going to take a lot of time and effort, my husband just didn't see it that way. Not having an eating disorder himself, he had a naive notion that taking certain steps would fix me overnight. When that wasn't happening, he became discouraged, which in turn created more frustration and animosity within our relationship. Feelings of defeat and despair surfaced within me. Why couldn't he understand that something so engrained in me over a period of ten years could not just go away in a matter of weeks or months?

Brad

BEFORE MEETING MY WIFE, my world was very black and white, right and wrong, and very rarely was there a gray area. It troubled me deeply to see someone who was a brilliant individual, well educated, and who had such a caring heart toward others, knowingly make such vain decisions, deny herself essential calories while suffering with constant hunger, and generally allow the opinions of strangers to drastically affect her self-worth. It was very hard to see her abuse herself, since I knew she'd find it unacceptable to treat others in this manner. It was almost as if abusing herself was acceptable and justifiable in some illogical way. I learned by going through this process with her that there are some gray areas in life that make rational individuals do irrational things.

Leigha

As a result of this early struggle, my therapist felt it best to involve my husband in the initial therapy meetings. By allowing this involvement, my husband was no longer hearing me preach about how I could get over the eating disorder, but rather heard factual statistics and reasoning from a trained professional who had the clinical knowledge to understand my situation. It also allowed him the opportunity to voice his opinion to a neutral third party, which was extremely important in his process of understanding.

In therapy, he was able to learn the best ways to support someone in the process of recovery. It was no longer about him trying to fix me. It became more about his support for *my own* recovery process.

He quickly learned not to judge my eating-disorder behaviors but rather help me talk through the emotions I was feeling that created the need for the behavior. He also learned to voice his recognition of improvement, rather than just point out when I fell back a few steps. This consistent and more positive approach led me to feel empowered and hopeful, which in turn helped me throughout my recovery process.

Brad

It was important for me to hear a professional tell my wife that these actions were unacceptable and self-destructive and that, if they weren't dealt with properly, would further destroy her self-worth and relationships with those around her. For a very long time she'd found every excuse to justify her abusive behaviors; however, hearing this information from the therapist, as opposed to me, turned on a light and made her want to get better.

For me, it was very beneficial to learn that the eating disorder was a smart and clever way to cope with a troubling event in her life. To me, this further reinforced that my wife was an intelligent person taking logical steps to deal with the pain in her past; however, the therapist was able to suggest healthier ways to deal with and manage the pain. I soon realized that the eating disorder was a symptom of a larger issue. As that issue was addressed, her need to continue the eating disorder slowly went away.

Daniel: Pulling Away

For love to triumph over ED, both partners need to recognize and accept that love involves intimacy. When one partner pulls inward, withdraws from emotional exposure, and is unable to relax and enjoy his or her own body, what's left for the other partner to do? In a sexual relationship the impact of an eating disorder can be particularly devastating because ED so often turns off the libido and erodes the trust required for sexual intimacy. These were the challenges that faced Daniel, a young husband whose wife has a history of anorexia and bulimia. When they were married three years ago, both believed she'd recovered. But although she seemed physically healthy, Daniel came to realize that the emotional underpinnings of her illness remained unchanged.

EVERYTHING WAS FINE while we were dating, then when we got engaged, things started to slide and continue to slide downward to this day. By "slide" I mean that she's gradually pulled farther and farther away from any form of intimacy.

Being married to someone who can't enter into intimacy is really, really tough, and I often think about divorce . . . not because I don't love her, but because she won't let me be her husband and she won't let herself be my wife. Essentially, we aren't married together . . . I find myself reaching out for her only to be rejected with a blank-stare sort of response. I want to be there for her, but I don't feel like I can do this much longer.

A JOURNEY IN INTIMACY
Suggestions for Partners and Spouses
By Cynthia M. Bulik

Eating disorders can threaten the relationships of even otherwise healthy couples. So often, partners are desperate to help and they'll try everything—not saying anything, nagging, yelling, eating with their ill loved one, even sacrificing their own health to help. But the most common refrain we hear is that partners simply don't know what to do. There's no playbook when your partner stops eating.

The best ways for partners to help are to

1. Educate yourself about eating disorders. Understand that these are not disorders of choice.

2. Learn to distinguish when your partner is talking and when ED is talking. Remember that your partner is separate from ED.

3. Keep in mind that recovery is rarely linear. There will be bumps along the road and it might feel as if it's one step forward and two steps back, but partner support is often listed by patients as the most important factor in recovery.

At the University of North Carolina at Chapel Hill we have developed an intervention for anorexia nervosa that leverages the power of the partnership and heals not only the eating disorder but also the relationship. Our program, Uniting Couples in the Treatment of Anorexia Nervosa (UCAN) (www.psychiatry .unc.edu/eatingdisorders/research%20eating%20disorders/ucan), brought together experts in eating disorders with experts in cognitive-behavioral couples therapy (CBCT). CBCT has been applied successfully to a range of medical and psychiatric conditions in order to bring the partner into the treatment experience. UCAN helps teach basic relationship skills, such as sharing thoughts and feelings and problem solving and, with that solid skill basis, deals with difficult issues such as eating together, eating with others, body image, physical intimacy, sexuality, relapse, and recovery. Our ultimate hope is that effective partner participation will lead to more lasting treatment gains and will remain a critical tool in preventing relapse.

Marie: In Sickness and in Health

Marie's letter shows the broad scope of relationships that are affected both by ED and by recovery. When Marie first wrote to me, she described herself as a "functioning anorexic" with a husband and four children. But after being in and out of treatment programs throughout her adult life, she'd finally reached her turning point and was determined to break her dependency. I was honored when she arranged for me to come and speak in her community. That evening I met an astounding group of supportive friends and relatives, including Marie's husband, who shared her recovery stage. A few weeks later, I was thrilled to learn that she'd begun to work with a gifted therapist who'd met her at that event. When I began to compile this book, I asked Marie to tell me a bit more about her friends and family members, how those relationships had come about, and how they've affected and been affected by her recovery.

I'M A FORTY-FOUR-YEAR-OLD WOMAN who's suffered from anorexia for more than twenty years. I've finally moved from a long time in the half life to real recovery. Why now? What has been my motivation?

I have four young children, I have a husband. They need me. I realized that I was missing so much of my children's lives. Until this year I'd never spent Christmas morning with my children. I was out running and they'd have to wait for me. I'd never eaten breakfast or lunch with my children. I'd never been able to travel far away from home, due to the constraints of my exercise and food routines. I'd never been able to eat lunches with girlfriends or celebrate with cake and ice cream. There were so many, "I never's"!!

The motivation to take a big step forward in my recovery came from a realization that my long-term therapist and I had hit a wall. I was too busy pleasing her to recover. I realized I needed to make a change in my treatment if I wanted to make progress. So, after thirteen years of working with her, I made the decision to leave and find new treatment.

This was not easy to do. But I saw that I was stuck, not making changes. I knew that if I had the flu and didn't get better, and the doctor kept giving me the same medicine, I'd switch doctors. Why shouldn't it be the same in therapeutic relationships?

My dear high school friend encouraged me to go with my head and heart, and make the change. When I met with my therapist to tell her of my decision, she responded with hesitation. She talked about her needs, her wish to see me at the finish line. The focus wasn't on what was best for me but rather on her bruised ego. I explained that my journey has included a combination of therapists, nutritionists, and treatment programs. Each has added a tool or part of the definition of my recovery. But it was time for the next step.

This past year working on recovery has been challenging. As I begin to unthaw, I see that not only are my spousal and familial relationships changing but so are my friendships. The old Marie was a pleaser at all costs. The happiness of others was primary in my life. Some of my friendships were unhealthy. Being a pleaser from a very young age to my father, mother, and other family members and friends took away my freedom to make choices that were right for me. As a young adult and throughout my middle age I'd align myself with friends who were controlling. I was so fearful of being disliked that I'd continue in these friendships.

An example: I ran several times a week with a woman who disliked me. She was jealous, controlling, and competitive. I'd come home tearful at things she said to me and start my day off with the residue of her angry, selfish comments. When I'd just about had enough, she would swoon and do something nice for me. I'd forgive and forget. She also viewed me as weak and sickly. As I journeyed into recovery, I began to feel intolerant of her selfishness and meanness. Coincidently, I had an injury that stopped my running completely. The timing of that injury helped me see how my approach to running and friendships was hurting me. I used the opportunity to get distance from both.

It can be invaluable to step back and judge what is healthy in a relationship and what is not. For the first time, I'm considering my own needs and feelings, what's right for me. For example, I was the superwoman at our local swim club where my kids swam. I did everything from ordering suits to running meets. I volunteered for every job, every week, even if my children weren't there. What if *I* weren't there? Would I be forgotten or not needed? How scary!!

This summer, my children were interested in other activities and not so much in the swim club. I didn't go to the swim club once. I knew that if I didn't make the break complete, I might never break this pattern. I discovered I didn't miss it at all, or the activities associated with it. I felt relieved and free.

This was true in my community involvements, too. I've realized that I was involved in many activities to fill the voids anorexia created. If I chaired or volunteered for this charity, it would make me special and worthy. People would think I was superwoman. I was running myself into the ground, using what little energy the anorexia spared me, sacrificing family time to fill the void. But I couldn't keep up the pace.

Now as I try to put the pieces of my self back together, I take the time to step back and observe which relationships or commitments should continue. Which ones bring me pleasure? Which are a burden? As of now I've remained active in two or three organizations and resigned from the others. In the process I've realized that many of the qualities that made me successful as PTO president could and would also make me a wonderful mother and a wonderful friend.

As the ice melts, I'm now able to really feel which friendships hurt or sting. When time is so precious, why waste it on people who don't respect or care about my feelings?

It's not easy to listen to myself without ED haunting me. I repeat a mantra that I am OK, and that the guilt and shame must fade. The healthy self becomes louder than the unhealthy self over time. Recovery is not at all like the isolation and shame associated with ED. It's much more powerful and rewarding. The choices are made by me, not the disease. So I practice asking, "Is this ED or me?" Knowing the answer to this question becomes very relevant to the choices I make about my social or personal life.

On various levels it's sad to see the time that has evaporated, the hours wasted on unhealthy relationships, both personal and philanthropic. The final level has been my awareness of some of the patterns in my marital relationship. Having gotten married seventeen years ago, I realize that the man I married fell in love with the sick Marie. Bless his heart, when he chose to marry me, he saw past so many of my addictions. Yet I was very anorexic. I was looking for someone to take me to a better place. I married a very successful man who also had his own issues of perfection and success. He was also challenged with intimacy. He'd take care of me and I would demand little intimacy from him. A perfect match for ED's Marie. I had little or no energy to partner with him. I was spending what little energy I did have to please him. He was CEO of a company, and while I was sick, he could be the CEO of me. He became the constant caregiver. If I were truly well, would he still want me?

Weeding through the intricacies of our relationship over the past months, I've tried daily to be his partner, not his daughter or employee. I am truly able now to give both physically and mentally to the marriage. I can communicate with openness and not anger. My husband is trying to make changes too. He's beginning to listen to the needs that have surfaced through my recovery.

"In marriage, you can only be controlled if you allow yourself to be controlled," my therapist says. The healthy self must actively express her voice, over and over.

Angela: Coming Clean

Angela has struggled with ED in various forms since she was thir-teen. By age thirty-eight, she was a divorced mother of three and worked as an administrative assistant. She'd been hospitalized for clinical depression, suicidal thoughts, and uncontrollable bingeing, but several months after her release she hit bottom again. She real-ized she needed to stop pretending that she had everything under control. She needed to accept the help that the people who loved her were eager and willing to offer.

AN ANGEL OF A FRIEND CAME to my rescue and convinced me that it was time to face the demons. I realized getting fat was not what I'd been afraid of all this time. I was afraid of facing my life unemployed, a single mother of three, with a mortgage and a big house to take care of by myself. I was afraid of my life.

I decided, after an agonizing morning of crying my heart out in the shower and begging God to take away ED, that I'd stick to my meal plan from that day forward no matter what. It finally sank in that the meal plan was key to getting my life back.

I told myself that I could not waste another minute on ED. I spent the weekend with my parents, coming clean with them that I hadn't been eating again. I asked them to make sure I stuck with my meal plan that weekend. I ate everything on schedule as if I were in the hospital again.

Monday I got back to the hospital and had honest discussions with my team. I got back on track with my nutritionist and decided that my therapist at the time wasn't right for me. I found a new one, and she's been an integral part of my recovery.

I committed myself to recovering for my sake and for the sake of my children. I started eating all my meals with my children again, cooking healthy, balanced meals for us all according to the meal plan. I made finding a job my number-one priority, after my kids, and set about looking for one as if it were a full-time job itself.

Amazingly, after only two months, I was offered a job at the university where I'd done my undergraduate work, a dream that I'd been seeking since I graduated in 1990. Shortly after I started my job, I began a relationship with a special man that wouldn't have been possible just a few short months earlier.

I don't know what I weigh now, probably the weight that I was so terrified of achieving last summer, the weight that I thought, once obtained, would be the death of me. Ironically, it's where my life began.

Hearing Concern, Accepting Support
Strategies for Listening
By Diann M. Ackard

Warning signs that you need help and support are often noticeable to others before you can recognize them yourself. Friends might comment that you don't seem your typical jovial self. Family members might observe changes in your weight. Coworkers may wonder if illness is the reason you're not performing as usual.

Maybe you find that your interest in other people, outside activities, or other meaningful pursuits has dwindled; or you might become aware that you aren't able to enjoy your social life to its fullest because others are gathering over a meal you aren't comfortable sharing. Perhaps a friendship or romantic relationship becomes strained or ends because the other person is overwhelmed by your eating issues.

The following three strategies can help you read the warning signs that your friends and family deliver, make sense of them on your own terms, and set the stage to regain your life:

1. Honor other people's concerns.
You don't have to agree with their worries about your health and well-being, but take a step forward by accepting that they care about you and that they're noticing something that causes unease.

2. Make a mental note (or better yet, keep a log book!) when others express their concerns about your well-being.
Friends, family members, business associates, teachers, class-mates, and even strangers may send you messages that indicate how much eating and weight concerns have taken over your life. If the worries that others bring to your attention start to mount, this is a signal for you to heed their warnings and reassess your priorities. When you receive similar messages repeatedly or from multiple sources, it's past time to give the issue your attention. Take the step to seek consultation with an eating-disorder treat-ment specialist to assess your condition and the type of help available to you.

3. Use the third-person voice.
Pretend that *you* are the person giving advice to a loved one walking in your shoes. Would you just stand back and let your loved one become rigid, isolated, sad, obsessed, and malnour-ished, or would you try to intervene? Consider what steps you'd urge *her or him* to take and where you'd suggest turning for support. Are others offering you similar advice? Why not adopt those same tactics to help yourself?

Sandra: It's OK to Ask

You just never know who's waiting in the wings to play a role in your recovery. From parents to partners to strangers, your world is undoubtedly richer and more supportive than ED would have you believe. This astonishing letter, from a forty-six-year-old who's been blind since birth and struggled with Binge Eating Disorder from the age of seven, reminds us to keep that casting call open. The key, Sandra has found, is to seek out people to help you who are willing and able to look beyond what's in front of their eyes.

WHY IS SOCIETY so blind to the fact that eating disorders have a multitude of variables—the *least of which* are the visual cues? About the only visual trigger I experienced was secondhand: from my (all sighted) family's weight phobia. While never easy, our journey toward recovery could hit far fewer potholes if our illnesses were not attributed to superficialities.

The seeds of my eating disorder were sown, I believe, after my extremely premature birth in the mid-sixties. At that time parents weren't allowed to touch their medically fragile children in incubators. I faced the double trauma of painful treatments and of isolation, which, I think, gave me a predisposition to seek out other sources of comfort, such as food, rather than reaching for people when the going got tough.

My eating disorder began to make its presence known when I was in first grade. Needing some recess periods for training in blindness skills such as Braille and adapted math and generally being less active than when I was younger probably contributed to the development of some baby fat, which, I think, could easily have been lost had my family, who were all food- and weight-obsessed, paid less attention to it. Instead, I was the one who was forbidden to have junk food, given smaller portions at mealtimes, and required to do calisthenics—boring for anyone, but especially a seven-year-old who just wanted to play. Because of the emphasis on my weight, I developed my own food and weight obsession at a very early age—*without any exposure to visual media.*

While pursuing a BA in Youth Ministry and later an MA in Blind Rehabilitation, I used food to cope with the stressors of academic life and, now away from the hovering eyes of my family, I gained a great deal of weight. Unable to find work right away, the unemployment rate among working-age blind people being 80 percent, I became even more invested in an unhealthy obsession with food and weight after graduation. On the positive side, this did scare me into the beginnings of a journey toward recovery through attendance at Twelve Step meetings.

While I ultimately found the Twelve Step groups too confining, helpful information about the dynamics of eating disorders still managed to penetrate. I also established a prayer partnership, through which I learned how to express emotions instead of using food to suppress and release them. My partner wholeheartedly shared my conviction that blindness is just an incidental statistic about my identity, not a fascination, a mystical attribute, or a detriment. She gave me a forum to vent some of my frustrations about the sighted population's fixation on my disability. And within that relationship I discovered much of how my eating disorder served me; for instance, it gave me a way to communicate my sense of normalcy. While blindness itself was no hardship for me, I felt constricted by the labels society placed on me and having the eating-disorder label was my way of asserting, "Look, I'm just one of the girls with a relatively common problem, *not* just the blind one."

Today, other aids to my ongoing pursuit of mental and emotional health include the following:

- Involvement in a community chorus. Not only has the musical involvement furthered my recovery, but even more striking is the way our conductor has managed to chip away at the wall that long separated me from others. Generally, I have a very hard time accepting compliments. I've constructed a hard shell against the well-meaning praise of much of the sighted population, which marvels that I can accomplish the simplest tasks yet doubts the ability of blind people to fully participate in the world of work. Somehow, in the nonthreatening atmosphere of performance, this guy has a gentle-yet-firm way of shaping our musical expression, and he genuinely and frequently celebrates our successes (large and small, as individuals in our personal lives and as singers with shared musical goals). I am taking his words in as nourishment to my spirit. The need to replace human nurturing with physical food, or with otherwise destructive relationships with food and weight, decreases as I allow his kindness to penetrate. I never thought I'd see that!

- God. I am grateful to him for everything and everyone he has brought into my life. While our relationship is not always smooth, I know, from the time of my conversion at sixteen, that he can change lives— even my seemingly intractable attitudes and behaviors toward food and weight.

I believe that the very thing I least desire (intimacy) is the thing that is most healing. I hope to return to school for an MSW, to further my credentials with the aim of becoming a counselor for people with ED, giving a face to those in the blind community who have EDs. I'm also looking for an ED therapist as well as a physician I can feel comfortable with as a true teammate, a doctor who has an interest in ED work and can go beyond the obvious concepts of weight management.

I shudder to think how much farther down the ED road I might have gone, were it not for the non-eating-disordered individuals and groups of other sufferers, and my God, who have been available for strength and courage, whether or not I was open to their healthy influence. They have reminded me to take heart and to realize that the somewhat daunting process of recovery isn't always what it seems!

THREE

Treatment

O NCE YOU'VE TURNED the corner and set the stage, you'll understandably want to know *how* to recover. Oh, for a single, fail-safe, one-size-fits-all prescription! Unfortunately, no one I've ever met knows of one. Think about it: there's no single way into an eating disorder, so how could there be a single way out?

What we do know is that full recovery usually requires the help of at least one empathic and experienced personal therapist. We also know that treatment tends to be most effective when it's begun early and involves professionals who specialize in eating disorders. By professional, I mean a doctor, psychiatrist, psychologist, social worker, or nutritional counselor who has special training in the treatment of eating disorders. Education and experience are important. However, what matters most is the level of trust, honesty, and insight that develops between you and your therapist. Remember, this relationship has to be strong enough to break your relationship with ED. So choose this person with care.

The right therapist will be someone who understands the problems ED poses but who can also see through ED and past the obvious issues of eating and weight, to understand *you*. Not every counselor or psychiatrist is right for every patient, so you may need to interview several candidates before finding the one who's best for you. Do not give up! And do try to remember that therapists are human beings, too. It's no more reasonable to expect your psychologist to be perfect than it is to demand perfection of yourself. In fact, what makes your therapist most effective in working with you may be her willingness to share her own vulnerabilities. As the letters in this chapter indicate, many of the professionals who work in the eating-disorders field themselves have histories of eating disorders. For some patients, knowing that the therapist has "been there" helps establish trust and openness.

Because eating disorders involve brain chemistry, nutritional imbalance, behavioral issues, identity and social conflicts, and often other psychological conditions such as depression, anxiety disorder, or post-traumatic stress, a multidisciplinary team approach is recommended. The team approach supplements the primary therapeutic relationship with medical doctors, dietitians, and other specialists, as well as support groups involving other patients.

Unfortunately, the same perfectionistic logic that empowers ED will insist that there must be a right way and a wrong way to recover, and that anyone who doesn't get the "right" treatment will be doomed to fail. When searching for a therapist or treatment team, or entering a treatment program, it's imperative to remember that ED lies. The truth is, there are all sorts of ways to recover, and the right treatment is whichever one helps you break ED's stranglehold on your body and your mind.

The more serious your illness, the more intensive the level of treatment you are likely to need. Some people need to enter a day treatment program for several weeks, while others may require an inpatient program for several months. Some do best working one-on-one with a single therapist on a weekly basis for several years. Others require a combination of medication and talk therapy, while still others may respond to a brief course of cognitive or behavioral therapy or other methods. In many cases, the first order of business is to stabilize physical health by nourishing the body and stopping self-abusing behaviors. Learning to eat and exercise well and mindfully are vital aspects of treatment. But treatment, ultimately, is about figuring out who let ED into your life, and why. Who, in other words, is the *real* you, and what do you *really* need to thrive?

Effective treatment begins a process of transformation that will continue long after therapy ends. The letters in this chapter by no means cover the full range of treatment approaches, but they do speak eloquently of the experience of personal recovery that therapy makes possible.

Alice: Behavior and Belief

> *Just to give us some perspective, Alice, now fifty-seven and long recovered, shared her memories of treatment back in the 1970s and mused on the mixture of luck and struggle required in those days to return her to health.*

I HAD ACTIVE restricting anorexia from 1971 to 1976. I responded to inpatient treatment in a then cutting-edge program as part of a government-funded double-blind study in the mid-1970s. At the time, anorexia and bulimia were treated as the same condition. The treatment I received, behavior modification (an approach that focuses on rewarding healthy behavior and punishing harmful behavior), sounds barbaric now. It didn't work for a lot of people, but it saved my life.

What worked for me was that it gave me the permission to eat and gain that I wouldn't give myself. By the time I did gain significant pounds, the mental acuity kicked in that allowed me to start to break the crazy belief system. My newly improved nutrition seemed to feed an improved cognitive functioning. And the spiral went upward instead of down. Of course, it took another ten or more years to start to feel fairly normal about food.

They did a ten-year follow-up in 1985. Going back there for testing set me off again, as if I had to prove that I could still do it. But not for long. Once I got home from the institutional environment, I found my way out again.

Tina: Person to Person

> *Tina had wrestled with anorexia for seven years, during which she worked with several therapists, yet she never felt a strong sense of connection with any of them. Then, at twenty-five, she met Diane, whom she described as "unmatched in her compassion and realness." Diane disclosed that she, too, had a history of eating disorders and, from that moment, their relationship was one of mutual trust and understanding.*

THIS SHARED EXPERIENCE allowed me to completely open up to Diane and to the process of real recovery. I'd lied and manipulated my way through therapy before, always nodding in agreement but then leaving the office to engage in the same unhealthy behaviors. Before Diane, psychologists or nutritionists who instructed me to add nuts to my morning cereal as a weekly homework assignment only scared me. In our sessions together, Diane never focused on food or weight, nor did she push me beyond my own limits for recovery.

Each week, I faithfully met with Diane (and a team of professionals) and faced my biggest fears: learning about and accepting myself for me. For years, I viewed my emotions as out of control and starved myself in an attempt to numb those feelings. In therapy now I engaged my emotionality and tried to understand and manage the unique characteristics I possess.

Diane also helped me internalize the concept of "good enough." I was always so patient and nurturing toward others, but never turned the same patience and love inward. I learned to set boundaries, to address my own needs, and to say, feel, and act true to myself.

I started a journal focused on my recovery, including the emotions, accomplishments, and setbacks I faced throughout the process. I talked and talked and talked to Diane and to my family; talking became a vital tool for me to break the cycle of using food to communicate or alter my thoughts and feelings.

It was initially challenging to reintroduce foods and allow signals of hunger and satiety. Yes, I binged fairly consistently throughout the first year of my recovery. I gained weight that made me, at the time, hate my changing (healthy) body. I questioned Diane about whether my body would ever adjust and she compassionately reminded me that it just needed reprogramming. I believed Diane because I knew she'd experienced the same issues.

MEDICAL INSURANCE
Facts about Coverage for ED Treatment
By Scott Crow

Inadequate insurance coverage can be a major obstacle when you're seeking treatment for an eating disorder. Many insurance companies resist paying for ED therapy at all, or else cover far less treatment than the medical literature and treatment guidelines recommend. In countries such as the United States, where there are many different payers for health care, coverage can vary widely from insurer to insurer, and from person to person.

The reluctance of insurers to adequately cover ED treatment arises primarily from stigma, due to a lack of awareness about ED's significance and serious health risks, and a shortage of proven effective treatments due to lack of funding for ED research.

To improve access to treatment and encourage research funding, professionals, lawmakers, and other eating-disorder advocates are working to educate those responsible for health care policy and provision. The development of more effective treatments for ED symptoms will encourage improved insurance coverage. So, too, will efforts to help insurers understand the relative cost of ED treatment. By comparison with treatment for secondary psychiatric or medical conditions that may result from prolonged and severe eating disorders, prompt and comprehensive ED treatment can be very cost-effective.

If you're having difficulty obtaining appropriate insurance coverage for ED treatment, try not to get discouraged. You have more power to influence your insurance provider's decisions than you may realize. Persistence works!

1. Thoroughly review your insurance plan so you understand your benefits.

2. Enlist the help of your treatment team in providing documentation to support your claim and/or request. A number of countries have developed "best practices," or guidelines for the treatment of people with eating disorders. Your team will be familiar with the guidelines in your area and can reference them in their documents.

3. Denial of coverage is not the end of the road. With the help of your treatment team, follow the process to appeal the denial. A well-planned appeal can often yield the coverage you need.

4. Seek resources in your region that can guide you in advocating for improved insurance coverage. Online help specifically on this issue can be found at www.edtreatmenthelp.org. Other sources of general information and advice can be found in the Resources list at the end of this book.

All third-party-payer health care systems grapple with costs—whether private for-profit, private not-for-profit, or government payers are involved. Therefore, it's critical that we continue ED advocacy efforts around the world. The AED, in partnership with other eating-disorder groups and key stakeholders, developed the World Wide Charter for Action on Eating Disorders, a patient/caregiver bill of rights (visit www.aedweb.org for the full text of the Charter). It's intended to be used to advocate for improved access to specialized care, reduced stigma, and improved quality of eating-disorder-treatment, research, and prevention around the globe. To get involved in the implementation of the Charter in your region or to sign on in support of the Charter, visit www.aedweb.org.

You First
Choosing the Right Primary Therapist
By Beth Hartman McGilley

Tina's letter reveals many of the key ingredients of a successful therapeutic relationship. Previous therapists had scared her with demands, but Diane met her where she was at and let Tina dictate the pace of healing. Tina's "faithful" attendance, and Diane's patient but active listening skills helped to create a secure, therapeutic environment from which Tina was able to face her innermost fear—getting real. And Diane's thoughtfully considered disclosure of her own ED history helped reduce Tina's shame and invoke trust and hope.

But as Tina found, the first therapist you consult is not necessarily the right one for you. Ironically, what's needed at the outset is what's likely the least comfortable thing to do: pay attention to and trust your instincts! Notice how long it takes for your call to be returned; how the therapist responds to your questions; and whether he or she seems genuinely interested in your desire to seek treatment. The first few therapeutic encounters, including the initial phone call, can reveal critical information about the therapist's healing qualities and compatibility with you.

The following three tips can help you make a successful choice:

1. While successful therapy depends on the quality of and collaboration within the therapeutic relationship, the therapy "belongs" to you. You're the expert on yourself, whereas the therapist is an expert in fostering recovery. At the outset, be clear with your needs and expectations for therapy and ask if the provider is comfortable and capable of meeting them.

2. You should know in three sessions if a therapist is the right fit for your healing journey.

3. If the therapist is not right for you, ask for the names of other providers who might be better suited to meet your needs.

Other relevant information to consider in your decision process includes:

What's the therapist's educational background and ED treatment experience? Professionals who treat ED require a high level of specialization and advanced training, and seasoned ED experts will welcome this query.

Does the therapist work as part of a multidisciplinary team? Eating disorder treatment typically requires a team of experts, including a family physician, psychiatrist, psychotherapist, and dietitian. Ask for information on other team members and their level of experience in ED treatment.

What is the therapist's treatment approach and philosophy? It is appropriate to inquire if the therapist is current with the scientific literature and utilizes the most reliable and established treatments and practices available.

How experienced is the therapist in working with clients of your age, gender, race, and ethnicity? Also, if your ED is linked to a history of athletics, trauma, or substance abuse, make sure the therapist has experience dealing with those pertinent issues, as well.

Does the therapist offer or recommend other forms of treatment that might help you, such as family or couples therapy, or group therapy? Eating disorders happen and heal in relationship. Family therapy for children and teens, and couples therapy for married adults are almost always essential for effective treatment. Group therapy can also provide a safe and vital source of additional recovery support.

How are patient needs covered when the therapist is out of the office? Make sure you're comfortable and familiar with the procedure, should the need arise.

What are the fees for treatment? Know whether the therapist accepts insurance, and when payment is expected.

Trust your body's cues and responses as you and your therapist get acquainted. Try to listen past your very normal fears about beginning therapy and discern if you hear a positive, compassionate, and confident voice in the prospective therapist. How the therapeutic connection begins can have a significant impact on what unfolds during treatment and on your experience of recovery.

Stephanie: Race and Recovery

Eating disorders don't occur in a vacuum. The same person who wrestles with ED must deal with a host of other cultural, social, familial, and sometimes racial forces that can hinder recovery. Stephanie, the author of Not All Black Girls Know How to Eat: A Story of Bulimia, *wrote about the role that race played in her initial reluctance to seek the help she needed.*

As a black woman suffering from bulimia, I learned early that race made it easy to hide my disease in plain sight. The stereotypical bulimic is white, middle class to upper middle class—not a black woman raised below the poverty line. So no one noticed that I'd eat enough food for a family of four, eventually excusing myself for a lengthy trip to the bathroom before returning bloodshot and ravenous. I was the invisible woman.

For a long time I believed that therapy was for weak or crazy people. I was socialized to believe that only white people did that. Telling my problems to a therapist and a group of people, white or otherwise, was a betrayal not only of my family but of my race.

I was raised to believe I needed to be the archetypal strong black woman in order to be successful and normal. That was so far out of my reach during my bulimia, but I believed like many of the women in my family that I needed to suffer in silence—get control or go to God. That thinking kept me isolated even more than the bulimia. I felt like a double outsider.

When I finally went into therapy I insisted that the therapist be black, like me. Eventually the center found a therapist fitting my one criterion. Other than skin color, she and I could not have been more different. She told me that women should always be "ladylike," no matter what. She even believed women should submit to plural marriages! Obviously, she had no understanding of eating disorders. She simply thought that the right diet was the answer.

Eventually, I let go of the color issue and found the therapist who would understand me and help me to recover and move forward in other areas of my life.

Steve: Feeding Body and Soul

When Steve, the cyclist and surfer who wrote about his turning point in chapter 1, began treatment for his anorexia, he wasn't sure what to expect. He still thought he had a "female's disease," and he wondered whether the same therapy that worked for women could possibly work for him. As Steve discovered, the answer is yes; the key ingredients for recovery transcend gender.

THERAPY ADDRESSED THE MAIN ISSUES, or underlying causes, of eating disorders—effective communication and being able to feel again. Having an eating disorder, you become numb to everything. You disregard everything your body tells you and you cannot empathize with anyone else. Learning to feel again is tough, but an essential part of recovery. Learning to express yourself is also paramount in recovery. When something upsets you, being able to put those emotions and ideas into words gets them out of your system. Instead of allowing negative thoughts and feelings to permeate your soul, effectively putting your emotions into words can help rid you of self-defeating and destructive behaviors.

In other recovery programs you hear of a Higher Power, and my Higher Power, Jesus, has been walking with me throughout my recovery. I understand that many people have their own beliefs, and this is not to influence or impose my beliefs on anyone else, but spirituality can be invaluable.

And although I believe ED's are not about the food, fear of food is something that needs to be conquered. Without going into extreme detail, the one nutritional practice that enabled me to surf the wave of recovery is called Intuitive Eating.

To understand the basic idea behind Intuitive Eating, think of how you ate when you were two, three, or four. You ate what your body yearned for without thinking about fat, calories, carbohydrate, fiber, and so on. You consumed the food to a point where you were comfortably satisfied and even left some on the plate if you were satisfied before it was totally gone. If it tasted good to you, you were on it; if you didn't like it, you wouldn't touch it. Intuitive eating gets you in touch again with what it is you truly like to eat, and how to taste food, all while being conscious of how you feel before, during, and after a meal.

Facing Food
Nutrition Counseling and Intuitive Eating
By Evelyn Tribole

When you're in the throes of an eating disorder, it's difficult to hear your body's normal appetite cues for hunger and fullness. In essence, your "satiety meter" stops working properly because ED has altered your mind-body biology. This can happen in a number of ways:

- Chronic food restriction slows digestion, which results in an early and prolonged sense of fullness.
- Anxiety triggers a neurochemical cascade affecting appetite, so hunger may become blunted when you worry about eating and weight.
- If you have bulimia, when you stop purging, you may experience temporary bloating, which distorts the sensation of fullness.
- If you're prone to binge eating, you may find it difficult to recognize moderate fullness, or the sense of having eaten enough.
- The chronic malnutrition that may develop with a prolonged eating disorder can cause symptoms such as food cravings, difficulty thinking, depression, irritability, and low energy, which further disrupt normal appetite cues.

In short, ED puts your body through nutritional trauma.

Nutrition Rehab: Meal Plans and Schedules of Eating

To recover, your body needs consistent, predictable nourishment with adequate calories and nutrients, *including essential amounts of fat, carbohydrates, and protein*. In the early stages of treatment, your willingness alone may not be enough to ensure that your body gets the nourishment it really needs.

Meal Plan. You'll need some type of eating plan, under the direction of a registered dietitian. This plan provides support in the same way a cast helps heal a broken bone. The cast provides structure until the bone is strong enough on its own, but it's not intended to be permanent. Similarly, a meal plan serves as structure and support until the damage is healed and body and mind are restored to healthy functioning, which usually means weight restoration. Your body needs to be adequately nourished, even if you can't yet feel normal hunger cues.

Schedule of Eating. Creating an eating schedule helps contain anxiety by establishing a predictable expectation of when you'll feed your body. Eating regularly helps foster internal rhythms that help your physical system gear up for digestion and maintain a normal blood sugar level. With time, gentle hunger cues will begin to emerge around your regular eating schedule.

Keep in mind that the occurrence of regular hunger cues varies and is determined by many factors:

- Duration of eating disorder
- Malnutrition severity
- Anxiety intensity
- Motivation for recovery
- Medication

The challenge is not only to hear the physical sensations of hunger and fullness, but also to learn how to respond appropriately to these cues. For most people, this means working through fears, beliefs, and rules about eating and nutrition with the help of a registered dietitian who specializes in eating disorders.

Then, once satiety cues are normalized, you can move on to Intuitive Eating, a form of normal eating.

Intuitive Eating

Intuitive Eating is attunement of food, mind, and body—with three core characteristics:

- Eating for physical, not emotional reasons
- Reliance on internal hunger and satiety cues
- Unconditional permission to eat

The ability to eat any food is an important component of recovery and of Intuitive Eating. This means being able to recognize that no one food, or one day of eating, can make or break your health or weight. Eating becomes emotionally neutral—without moral dilemma, shame, or guilt. Consequently, it's easier to be attuned to the needs of your body.

Studies show that Intuitive Eaters eat a wider variety of foods, are more optimistic, and have better self-esteem and healthier body weights than dieters who strive to control their eating to achieve a thin ideal. New research also indicates that Intuitive Eating may be effective in the treatment of Binge Eating Disorder.

Ultimately, recovery means that you're at peace mentally and physically, and can enjoy the pleasures of eating. But this will take time. Be patient and have compassion for yourself and your body during this journey.

Brittany: Stepping into Treatment

Brittany had grown up believing that her identity was secure—because she was a triplet. She was even closer to her sisters than other girls are to their mothers or best friends. They completed her. It never occurred to her that this closeness could have a downside, but when she married and her husband got a job in a different state, she had to separate her own identity from those of her sisters. She became severely depressed, and that's when her eating disorder began. One of the biggest obstacles to recovery was her reluctance to accept psychological treatment.

MY SWEET, LOVING HUSBAND wanted to help but did not know how. I felt like I was failing and began to isolate myself from everyone. I felt like I'd lost myself and had no desire to try to make new friends. I remember writing a short e-mail to my sisters and mom that said, "I can't remember a day that I have not cried. I'm scared. Please help me."

I had to see a therapist—an idea I dreaded. I knew what the problem was: I was one of three, and now I felt like nothing. What could some therapist tell me that would make me feel differently? Also, I was so scared that she would suggest I needed medication.

I saw several therapists. Because I could never finish and get the words out, my mother-in-law came with me and told my story (she'd struggled with an eating disorder as well, when she was first married). I felt each time that the therapists were just writing down notes and trying to fix the problem. They all diagnosed me with severe depression and anorexia, which I couldn't understand because I was sure I didn't have either! I was just a little sadder than normal, I thought. I was very angry after leaving my therapy sessions and felt even more desperate, thinking I was always going to feel miserable. Then I found G.

I walked into her office and instantly felt that she really listened to me. At the end of our first session, G turned to me and said what changed my life: "You don't have to live like this."

I worked with her for weeks, as she listened patiently and asked questions about my past. I remember getting angry one time with her when she said that being a triplet was a big part of who I was, but not *who* I was. I wanted to yell, "Being a triplet defines me! I will not be happy without them!"

That's when I decided to take the dreaded antidepressant. After talking *a lot* about how the mind works, I began to understand that medicine is necessary for some people in order to help the brain change and get rid of the depression.

I sat self-consciously in the psychiatrist's waiting room. She was extremely cold (or so I thought) and said some things that were harsh. (Obviously she did not know how to talk to someone as sensitive as me!) I walked out of that office and into the arms of my sweet sister, crying, "I will never go back to her," and I didn't.

I went instead to my family doctor, and explained everything. He prescribed the medicine, and I was scared to take it, but after I started and realized that I'd gone one week without crying, I began to feel more hope.

Then it was two weeks without crying. I began to feel more in control of my life. I could do the things G asked me to do, thinking that they'd help me and that I did deserve it.

I realized that my whole life I was unique by being a triplet. All I had to do was walk with my sisters to be noticed and stared at . . . . Then all of a sudden I was alone and had never felt more invisible or insignificant. I'd never found out who I truly was—because my sisters compensated for my weaknesses. Moving away forced me to figure out who I was too quickly, causing me to lose myself completely.

I've realized that ED was not my fault and is something I can learn from. I'm so glad that I put away my embarrassment and took the necessary step in asking for help. I began to realize my self-worth. I found myself wanting to go out and be with others. Eating became less of a concern for me. I was finally happy!

I'm still taking the medicine. I was so against it, but some people need it to help rewire their brains. I am so thankful that I decided to take the step.

MEDS AND ED
The Role of Medication in Eating-Disorder Treatment
By Mark Warren and Ovidio Bermudez

Recovery depends on identifying and addressing the specific circumstances that have created the ED. That's why the most effective treatment approaches are primarily behavioral and psychological. Medication alone can never cure an eating disorder, and the decision to use psychiatric medication as part of your treatment requires careful consideration. Some people welcome the possibility that a medication will provide some relief to their misery (and they are likely to ask that it be included in their treatment). For others, the idea of medication is more complicated. There may be a sense that one should be able to get better without medications, that their use represents a form of weakness, or that taking them implies some deeper illness that the individual doesn't feel she or he has. Sometimes there's a sense that medications are not natural or could be dangerous. Sometimes trusted loved ones, the media, or other sources recommend against medication.

In these situations, as in all others related to eating disorder treatment, it's crucial to work with a medical professional you can trust, one who is part of an integrated treatment team that will work with you to ensure that you receive the best care and have access to all options that may relieve your suffering. Negotiating the maze of treatment choices is easier with someone who knows the following: when medication makes sense and when there are other options, which medications are evidence-based, which may put you at risk, and which are most likely to do no harm.

Scientific evidence shows that medication may play three valuable roles in treatment and recovery:

1. *For ED symptoms:* Medication is most often prescribed to help reduce bulimic purging. Studies have shown that in about 50 percent of patients with bulimia, Prozac or an equivalent selective serotonin reuptake inhibitor (SSRI) will lower both purging behaviors and the urge to purge. In combination with behavioral and psychological treatment, the response rate is much higher. Usually, Prozac needs to be prescribed at high doses (60 mg) to be effective.

No medication—other than healthy doses of nourishing food—has been shown effective in treating the malnutrition that can result from anorexia and bulimia, nor has medication been shown effective for any other eating-disorder behaviors.

2. *For co-occurring symptoms:* More than half of all patients with eating disorders also suffer from anxiety and/or depression, and medications can be very useful in treating these conditions. Benzodiazepines (Lorazepam, Alprazolam, Clonazepam) help reduce anxiety. And SSRIs (Fluoxetine, Sertraline, Citalopram) are helpful for both anxiety and depression. People with EDs often find it reassuring to know that these medications don't cause either weight gain or weight loss. However, SSRIs tend to be less effective in patients with extremely low body weight.

The stronger, second-generation antipsychotic medications (SGAs—Quetiapine, Olanzapine, Aripiprazole, Risperidone) are also useful for anxiety and depression with eating disorders. These medications have more side effects, but they also have two significant advantages. First, they are more potent and may help ease the intensity of feelings and thoughts in eating disorders when other medications do not. Second, people even at low body weights may respond well to SGAs.

3. *For secondary physical discomfort:* Medication can help with the gastrointestinal discomfort and other physical symptoms that many people experience during the early stages of recovery. For example, as laxative abuse is interrupted, slow functioning of the colon may become a problem and certain medications can help reestablish bowel function. As they stop purging, some people also experience fluid retention and edema, which may require treatment with medication. And both underweight patients who increase their food

intake and individuals who stop purging may have digestive difficulties that can be relieved by antacids and pro-motility agents (medications that stimulate emptying of the stomach).

If you're recovering from an eating disorder, make sure that any medication you take, including over-the-counter remedies, is prescribed and monitored by an experienced clinician. If you wish to pursue the use of alternative treatments in addition to or instead of using medication, be aware that we have little research to guide the consumer in the use of these approaches. Again, consult your treatment team and other reliable resources regarding the use of approaches that have not been thoroughly studied in regard to their treatment effectiveness.

Pam: Beyond Symptoms

For Pam, whose ED was intertwined with childhood trauma and a legacy of eating and substance-abuse disorders in the family, effective treatment required far more than medical and nutritional support. After several lengthy hospitalizations and stays in treatment programs before she was twenty-two, she came to understand that recovery depends on confronting and healing the true source of the ED.

I THINK WHEN CENTERS approach symptoms first, they fail.
"OK, you won't eat, I'll put a tube up your nose. "
"OK, put a tube up my nose, I'll pull it out."
"You eat this Boost."
"No, I'll just sit here."
This is the wrong approach. The harder you fight the disorder, the harder it fights back.

But treat the underlying reason (or at least find it), and then the symptoms will fall away. When you nurture and build up the real person behind the disorder, the disorder gets smaller and smaller and less needed.

Perhaps when they say these disorders are reaching out for attention, they are, but not the attention people think. Most people with EDs want any kind of attention, good or bad, because they're lonely, terrified, small, and they need to be held. Except they think their disorder does that for them, and it doesn't.

I spent so long trying all the wrong things to gain love, affection, and praise. In treatment my biggest fear was that when and if I wasn't sick, these people would leave me, that no one would love me when I wasn't sick because they wouldn't need to.

That's a fear I saw in people at all stages of treatment. But if you can convince people they're loved more when they're *better*—when they're *not* a patient—I think they will recover.

Liana: It May Take a Team

> *Liana wrote her letter three years after completing treatment. In her home country, Estonia, she'd seen many individual therapists over the five years when her eating disorder was active, but none had been able to help her. Finally, her health so deteriorated that she feared she would die. In her early twenties she enrolled in a hospital treatment program in Germany.*

WHEN I WAS PACKING my things, I planned to be in hospital for six weeks, but in reality my treatment lasted much longer. The clinic used a cognitive-behavioral approach, which consisted of nutritional, art, group, individual, and other therapies. Besides that, I was with fifty other patients all willing to get better. I was not alone.

Every day at clinic was a struggle. Gaining weight was easy, but accepting that gain was a fight. Many nights I cried myself to sleep, many times I wanted to run away, go back to a life where I felt in control and safe; but the feelings I started to feel, the love I saw around me, and the feeling of being myself again—actually seeing somebody I recognized in the mirror—made me fight.

I gained much more than I expected, and I panicked, since I was eating healthily, being active, and yet still gaining. But I kept reminding myself, it's all part of my recovery.

I remember in clinic when, for the first time in five years, I actually felt the feeling of happiness. I had been in treatment for three weeks. I was sitting next to an open window, breathing fresh early-morning air, looking at birds flying past the rising sun and listening to the silence. I suddenly felt *happy*. The feeling was so overwhelming, I cried. I felt alive.

I left the clinic after fourteen weeks, having gained all the weight I needed up to a minimum healthy BMI. I actually felt that I was ready to go back into life.

During the year that followed, my body tried hard to adapt to my new weight. I still felt blue at times, but I met a very dear person who simply adored my body and my personality. He helped me over the hard times and supported me as much as he could. We have now been together for over two years and I have never been happier or felt more feminine in my entire life.

CBT for Eating Disorders
Cognitive-Behavioral Therapies
By Myra J. Cooper and Wayne A. Bowers

People with eating disorders often use their weight or body shape as a measurement of their personal value. They'll think, "If I gain weight, then no one will want me," or "If I'm unattractive, then others will despise me." Other typical comments reflect a negative self-image: "I'm repulsive," or "I'm disconnected from everyone." Research suggests that issues of self and identity play an important role in ED, so these thoughts, and not only weight, shape, and eating, must be addressed in therapy.

Cognitive-behavioral therapies (CBT) can teach you how to replace such negative self-talk with more rational, helpful statements. CBT assumes that certain thought patterns and attitudes contribute to problematic eating behavior and emotional distress. The goal of therapy, then, is to shift thinking into more constructive patterns that help reduce binge eating, restricting, depressed mood, and anxiety.

CBT therapists typically will begin by "formulating" or developing a good understanding of your problems and working out which beliefs and thoughts best explain, contribute to, and maintain your eating disorder. They'll be interested in your views on the therapy, including the quality of each session and how the treatment is proceeding. They'll also be keen to build a strong and collaborative relationship with you, as this is the foundation of recovery.

Some forms of CBT focus more on changing behavior; others focus more on changing attitudes. To accomplish these goals, a CBT therapist may use one or more of the following:

- Verbal strategies, such as recording and responding to thoughts on a "thought record sheet."
- Behavioral strategies, such as assignments or exercises designed to objectively test your beliefs or expectations in everyday life.
- Experiential strategies, such as exercises involving images and memories from the distant past or body sensations and feelings.

CBT is generally delivered as individual or group psychotherapy. However, CBT self-help, where you work on a program by yourself or with more general guidance from a therapist, can also be effective. Individual or group therapy is most likely to be needed if your eating disorder is moderately severe, or if it doesn't improve following self-help. Treatment can be tailored to any stage of recovery, and research has found CBT to be particularly effective with bulimia nervosa.

Merry: Deconstructing DBT

Merry had suffered from anorexia, depression, and posttraumatic stress disorder (PTSD) for decades. In spite of her illness, she had a strong marriage of thirty years and two healthy sons. Also, she was a registered nurse. But neither her family support nor her training as a nurse was enough to beat her eating disorder. Then, at fifty-one, she entered a treatment program that offered dialectical-behavior therapy, or DBT.

DBT is a method that combines standard cognitive-behavioral techniques with practices emphasizing mindfulness, interpersonal effectiveness, emotion regulation, distress tolerance, and acceptance. These practices are based on Buddhist meditation, which researchers have found can physically change the brain in ways that make people happier, healthier, and more peaceful. Why Buddhist meditation specifically? Because Buddhism as a philosophy equates perfection not with rigid standards or measures but with the more open-ended ideal of insight. Also, the explicit goal in the practice of Buddhist meditation is to achieve release from suffering. According to this philosophy, every one of us is entitled to question values and assumptions that contribute to our suffering and to replace them with values and assumptions that enhance peace, compassion, and well-being. These principles are all incorporated in DBT, which has proven over the past decade to be effective in treating a variety of self-harming syndromes, including bulimia and anorexia.

Merry also found she needed the intensive help of a residential program that offered a team of specialists. Her recovery really swung into high gear when she grasped the central dialectic (or contention) of DBT: "You are doing the best you can, and you can do better."

I FOUND IT HELPFUL to think of everyone on my treatment team as teachers trying to help me learn about life in a different way, instead of being health care providers examining me. I learned that *trust* is not just an empty word. And I realized that there are some genuinely kind people in this vast world.

My therapist was a lesbian with spiked blond hair and a gruffness about her. When I overcame my fear of her, I was able to accept her kindness. She told me healing was like crossing a raging river by hopping on stones to the other side. The beach on the other side was a place of peacefulness and personal self-acceptance. I had to cross that river without help, without a life jacket, and not knowing how to swim. Once moving forward, it was impossible to move backward onto a previous stone. When I fell off a rock, I had to find my own power to climb back on. I was able to let go of perfection by understanding that mistakes are an opportunity to learn something new.

One crucial lesson for me was that I mattered. I thought I was different from other people, more like an inanimate object than a woman. I thought the reason I was alive was to please others. I thought if people were nasty to me or if they physically or emotionally hurt me, it was OK because they'd feel better about themselves. I didn't know that I was as valuable as everyone else.

It was a shock to learn that I wasn't feeling feelings like other people. I'd been using restricting and dissociation to numb or avoid feelings. Now I'm learning to put names on these unfamiliar feelings. My psychologist taught me to cope with their intensity by visualizing ocean waves flowing onto a beach, peaking for a moment, and then receding back into the ocean.

DBT states that there's always more than one way to see a situation and always more than one way to solve a problem. I felt a change happen when I began to question my own thinking and reactions. *Was* there actually a right way to be? Could a good day begin *without* stepping on a scale? Were my expectations too high to achieve? Was there such a thing as being good *enough*? Was I a marionette just *pretending* to be alive?

These questions made me wonder if I was looking for the answers in the wrong places. Using the DBT skill of mindfulness, I began asking myself questions without judging myself. Was I trying too hard at everything? Was I wasting a lot of my life without knowing it by clinging to harsh internal judgments? Was I spinning my wheels by trying to run away from feelings? Was there such a thing as peace inside of me? Where did happiness hide? Why did some people seem to have life so easy? How could I know when enough was enough? Was it possible that my care providers were right in stressing that ED was lying to me? The answers I needed were not external. I needed to search inside.

I focused on coping in a more healthy way, by just being in the moment, for example, noticing the sensation of air entering my lungs, my chest softening with a longer slow breath outward, relaxing my tight shoulders, and feeling the parts of my body touching the chair.

Mindfulness made it easier to get in touch with emotion by letting go of harsh self-judgments. I try not to use the word *should* because it puts pressure on me to be different than I am, setting me up for failure. I am good enough.

Progress continued when I began getting curious about my thoughts, feelings, and judgments. The first step was to stop and be more mindful of the thoughts in my head, the internal voices beating up my soul. I tried to put a small wall of space between me and my critical judgments by focusing on the language I was using. For example, instead of saying, "I'm fat," I'd say, "I'm aware I'm thinking, 'I am fat. I am stupid. I am bad. I am worth-less.'" I'd say, "Isn't that interesting? Hmmm . . . I wonder why that is?"

I was able to observe the thoughts I was having as if I were watching a stranger. It meant just sitting with the feeling, sitting with myself in that moment, not beating myself up, or trying to fix things. It took a lot of energy. I moved forward by just noticing that when I have a negative thought, it has the power to continue on to another negative thought, growing bigger and bigger. Pretty soon I can find myself caught up in misery so profound that I'm locked into my own hopelessness. But DBT helped me see that this thought pattern doesn't mean I'm bad. I learned to say to myself, "It just is."

It happens to all of us. We can get into such a vulnerable emotional state that we can't think rationally. Some people go on a huge binge when in this state, eating everything in the fridge. Some people find solace in drinking or numbing themselves with drugs. I found comfort in not allow-ing myself to eat. Restricting provided me with a false sense of control.

I was able to notice when I was having a negative thought and what preceded it. That gave me something to work with so I could soften my pain and limit its power. My therapist coached me to cope with feelings in a healthier way by using distress-tolerance techniques, distracting my mind toward things I enjoy, such as listening to music, sewing, or enjoying nature. I found there's hope!

At the treatment center, affirmations were used in groups and were posted on walls. Initially I thought they were just empty words. Now I know that our thoughts affect our feelings, and our feelings affect our behavior. I try to say some positive things about myself every day. The positive words eventually penetrate so that I'm able to believe them.

It was difficult to tolerate my own humanness. Patience with others is easy, but not patience with myself. I'm a highly driven person who must accomplish things in a very organized manner. I wanted to feel completely healed in an instant. It had to be perfection. But progress couldn't be forced.

My nutritionist told me that my perceptions of my body would be more accurate after I gained some weight. She was right. When I follow her food plan, she's able to keep me at a healthy weight that we've both agreed on. She's teaching me what lowers or increases my metabolism. My medications feel more effective now that I'm at a healthier weight. I'm not feeling depressed.

From time to time, I still fall off the rock into the river, but am able to find the ability to crawl back on without a life jacket, without help, and without knowing how to swim. I still find myself draped over the top of the rock totally exhausted at times. But the experience teaches me. DBT skills have given me a new life.

> *After Merry began to face and manage her true feelings, she gained the strength to confront an experience buried deep in her past, which her eating disorder had suppressed. This process was frightening, but also fascinating. More to the point, it was essential for her full recovery.*

AFTER LEARNING TO LET GO of some of my need for perfection and give myself permission to slow down by being more mindful, hidden feelings began to slowly emerge and my personality fragmented. I have at least ten little girls inside of me. They held the answers to my struggle with anorexia.

Now when I feel the little girls inside me, the adult part of me has control. It feels spooky, since one speaks baby Canadian-French, and I don't know how to speak French. But it was a primary language of my grandparents when I was under the age of four, and my grandparents raised me. The little girls are telling me my story of physical and sexual abuse. Now I know why I've been so sick with PTSD and anorexia. I have something to work with.

My treatment team is helping me to learn containment, to soothe the little girls inside of me, and to integrate them into core being. I'm in a wonderful place, trying to soak up every moment I have left in my life to make up for the years when I just existed.

Making Peace with Pain
DBT in the Treatment of Eating Disorders

By Lucene Wisniewski

Dialectical-behavior therapy (DBT) was originally designed to help patients suffering from Borderline Personality Disorder (BPD), a form of mental illness characterized by extreme moods, intense emotions, troubled relationships, and poor self-image. People with BPD are often prone to self-injury and suicidal thoughts and urges, but Marsha Linehan, who developed DBT in the late 1970s, found that these urges are linked to core difficulties in managing emotions. She observed that people with BPD use self-harming behaviors to make negative emotions more tolerable in the short term. In the long term, however, these behaviors created other more serious difficulties. The treatment she developed therefore focuses on helping people manage their emotions more effectively.

Over the past decade or so, DBT has been adapted for use with eating disorders. The research on this treatment suggests a good fit: studies have shown DBT to be effective with bulimia nervosa and binge eating disorder, and new research indicates it may be effective with anorexia nervosa, as well.

How can DBT help you overcome ED?

DBT teaches you to use safe and constructive skills, rather than eating-disorder behaviors, to manage your emotions. These skills include the following:

- Emotion-regulation techniques designed to make emotions more manageable and less overwhelming
- Mindfulness skills that can help you experience and better identify your true emotions
- Distress-tolerance skills, which help you manage the discomfort of intense emotions without engaging in potentially harmful behaviors
- Interpersonal-effectiveness skills, which help you to communicate effectively and build more secure relationships

DBT also teaches a nonjudgmental stance. People with eating disorders are often judgmental of themselves and their choices as well as the way they look and how much they weigh. The judging leads to a spiral of self-recrimination that can get you stuck. For example, if you're very critical about how you handle a particular problem, talking about the problem will make you feel guilt and shame, so you'll avoid talking about it. This pattern of avoidance makes it less likely that you'll find a solution or better way to approach the problem next time. DBT teaches you to consider your behavior and experiences without judging them, so you can solve problems more quickly and effectively.

Recovery from an eating disorder can take years and may therefore call for sustained commitment. DBT strategies can help motivate you to stay in treatment. Also, issues of trauma may surface that need to be addressed during treatment. Therapy for trauma becomes more effective once you've replaced eating-disorder behaviors with DBT skills as a way of coping with the memory of traumatic events.

Beth: The In-between

The first months of treatment are often scary and unpredictable. As ED's false security is broken wide open, hope can fire up, fade, and flare again without warning. Nerve endings are exposed. The body changes and old habits give way. Identity becomes an ominous question mark. Beth's letter highlights one of the most difficult but essential practices during this first phase of recovery: waiting.

EXISTING IS ELEMENTARY, but it takes practice. In very early recovery, I needed to be told exactly what to do. As a matter of fact, I disengaged from any suggestions that placed responsibility on *me* having to make decisions. ED still had too much power over my thoughts, and thus, I had to stay highly guarded against it. I was either 100 percent in recovery or in relapse. Black and white. All or nothing.

There *was no in-between*. I cannot think of a better description of ED. I'm only now starting to understand that the advice I've been given— through therapy, treatment, support groups, and talking with other sufferers—is not set in stone. I think this has been one of the hardest things about recovery, the fact that it is *not* black and white. What works for someone else may not necessarily work for me, nor can I put a time limit on this process.

Comparing myself to others, whether in terms of sickness or recovery, is a recipe for disaster. My eating disorder developed from an affliction inside me; thus, my recovery process is a blueprint for healing the specific demons within me.

I'm currently in the interim period of this transformation. The in-between is slow, but I'm learning to trust that waiting is one of the most productive practices in recovery.

Julie: Letter to ED

Julie had tried to hide her eating disorder for fifteen years when she finally entered a specialized day-treatment program at age twenty-eight. During the first year after treatment her relapses were so frequent that she described her experience as a recovery roller coaster. But gradually her relapses became less severe and occurred less often. When ED's thoughts and urges were strong, Julie found she could fight them by rereading the letters her therapist had had her write to ED while in treatment.

I JOURNAL A LOT and stay in touch with my therapist throughout the week by e-mail. When I'm struggling, reading the entries from when I was stronger in recovery reminds me how much better things can be. One of my therapy assignments was to write a letter to my eating disorder stating what ED has taken from me. I carry this letter with me, to remind myself why I'm fighting so hard to stay in recovery.

> Dear ED,
> You have been the one constant in my life. When others let me down, I can always turn to you and know you'll be there for me. When things get too hard, you're my escape. When I hurt, you numb me out. I thought I had control over you, but the truth is, you've had control over me. Now I still struggle to get that control back.
>
> I lose more than weight with you. I lose the ability to have feelings and emotions. When you're strong, all I feel is depressed and anxious. I have to put on a front for everyone else and keep you a secret while feeling like I'm dying inside.
>
> I've lost time to you. When you are strong, staying faithful

to you is very time-consuming. I hide behind you, rather than dealing with the issues in my life. You convince me I need to stay committed to you, rather than develop dreams of my own. Now I have years and years to catch up on. It's an ongoing battle, between you and me. I don't know who I am without you.

I've lost energy to you. When you are strong, I have to fit in a certain amount of time for exercise. It doesn't matter if I'm exhausted from a full day at work, or that my body aches from being worn down and deprived of proper nutrition. I continue to put my body through hell and run it into the ground, yet somehow it keeps going. I don't know the true feelings of hunger and satiation.

I've lost the ability to think clearly and concentrate. When you are strong, all I do is obsess about food, calories, and weight rather than thinking about more important things. My worth depends on a number. It's hard to have a moment of peace in my head without you berating me for the way my clothes fit, my size, weight, looks, and so on.

I've lost relationships. When you are strong, too many times, I choose you over others. I don't want others to know about my relationship with you. You make me moody and irritable, so no one wants to be around me, and I don't want to be around others.

I've lost the ability to go out to eat and enjoy myself. When you are strong, I can't go because you convince me it's better to isolate because socialization involves food.

I've lost my integrity. When you are strong, I have to lie for you and cover my tracks. I don't like you, but I have a hard time letting you go.

Another therapy assignment was to write about what life would be like without an eating disorder. Again, I carry this with me, to remind myself why I'm fighting so hard to stay in recovery.

What would life be without ED?

- Waking up each morning and looking forward to the day
- Having energy to get through the day without feeling dizzy or exhausted
- Having the ability to concentrate and think clearly
- Having healthy hair that doesn't fall out
- Not having to keep my nails painted so others don't see they're blue
- Being warm
- Not panicking if my pants feel tighter
- Not feeling guilty after I eat or immediately trying to find time to exercise to compensate for eating
- Not obsessing about food, calories, and weight
- Not allowing the number on the scale to determine what kind of day I'm going to have
- Feeling comfortable with myself and not always comparing myself to others
- Not dwelling on the past or worrying about the future
- Having the ability to handle my emotions
- Dealing with problems instead of trying to deny them and numb the pain
- Not feeling so ashamed and embarrassed about who I am
- Having the ability to forgive myself and trust myself
- Not blaming myself for everything or feeling responsible for all the problems in the world
- Realizing that I have support and cannot get through this alone, nor do I need to
- Believing that I don't have to be perfect
- Realizing that the hardships and pain of recovery are worth the end result
- Having hope

Finally, I try to be patient with myself, because recovery is a process.

NOTES TO SELF, LETTERS TO ED
The Benefits of Journaling and Letter Writing

By Lucy Serpell

Many people with eating disorders find writing journals and personal letters to be a useful therapeutic tool. In these private writings you can tell your truth without fear of criticism or invalidation. You can release your thoughts, then examine them objectively on the page. In this way, you can help to distinguish the words that ED puts in your head from the voice that belongs to the healthy, true you.

You might start by keeping a diary of thoughts, feelings, and situations that occur when you eat, drink, restrict, or exercise. When you're in ED's grip, eating, skipping meals, bingeing, and overexercising are usually accompanied by powerful thoughts and emotions. Tracking these links in writing not only can reveal the thoughts and feelings that trigger ED, but it can also help you change your responses to those thoughts and feelings. For example, if you notice that you often respond to anger by bingeing, try writing through the anger before turning to food, and then see if the urge to binge is still as strong. Use the act of writing to think through other ways you might express or relieve your anger that are less destructive—and perhaps more effective than ED.

You can also write letters to bring ED into perspective. Try writing to your eating disorder, first as a friend and then as an enemy. It's helpful to write the two letters separately so that you can concentrate fully on the good things and the bad things that ED has given you. Once you've written them, have a good look at the results, sharing them with your therapist if you have one.

Start by looking at the pro-ED letter, which may reveal your reasons for maintaining the disorder, as well as the "benefits" that must be given up in recovery.

A few questions to consider:

• What are the most powerful attractions of the eating disorder?
• How do they make you feel?

- What would it be like to lose those effects?
- Could you get the positive effect of the eating disorder some other way? (For example, if one of the good things about the eating disorder is the feeling of being good at something, could you get this benefit from something else in your life, such as a hobby, relationships, work, or study?)

Now turn to the cons of the eating disorder, such as the health risks of being underweight or repeatedly bingeing and vomiting. These can be scary to contemplate, but consider . . .

- What are the most powerful downsides of the eating disorder?
- How do they make you feel?
- What would it be like to lose those negatives?

Notice whether the pros and cons are mainly short-term, long-term, or a mixture of both. It's common for the pros to be quite immediate and the cons more long-term, making it tempting to ignore the cons in favor of short-term benefits. But consider what this will mean for your life as a whole. Where will you be in five years if you still have the eating disorder? How about if you recover?

This line of inquiry can generate another useful exercise:

Write two letters, either to ED or to a trusted friend, imagining yourself five years from now. In the first letter, imagine that ED is still with you. Describe how this future life of yours is going. How are your relationships, work life, and emotional life? How are your mood and physical health being affected by a long-term ED?

Then write the second letter imagining that it's five years in the future and you've recovered. Again, how is life going? What are your interests, your pursuits? Don't forget to mention the challenges of living without ED, as well as the benefits.

Recovery, of course, involves more than simply weighing the pros and cons and deciding to get better. But letter writing and journaling can help you gain motivation and strength for the task ahead. Like Julie, you may want to keep these documents close at hand to refer to as a source of hope and perspective as you move forward.

FOUR

Restoration

IN MANY WAYS, an eating disorder mimics a cruel and jealous parent who promises protection but delivers enslavement. Life with ED feels like a traumatic childhood from which there is no escape. Recovery, then, can be likened to a delayed—but healthy—adolescence.

As with actual adolescence, the first phase of individuation is bound to be messy, painful, and unsettling, but it's also exciting and full of promise and surprise. If the initial break with ED occurs during treatment, then the phase of recovery that follows treatment allows you to return to your senses—to feel your body, experience emotion, sense the world, and re-connect in healthy ways with the people who love and care about you. Being liberated *from* ED means being liberated *to* a wide-open and new kind of existence. Making sense of this new way of being, and learning how to find meaning and direction on your own terms, is the work of this phase, which I call restoration.

This is the time to restore body and mind while phasing ED out of your life. Healthy dreams and desires need to replace the fixation on food and weight. New goals, new forms of creativity, and self-expression need to replace the habits of restriction, numbing, and self-abuse. And genuine human relationships need to replace your relationship with ED.

This transformation won't happen quickly or easily. Why not? Kim Lampson, a psychologist who broke free of her eating disorder some twenty years ago, compares the process to physical therapy: "There was a story in *People* magazine about a man who severely injured his arm but was so determined to use his limb again that he worked for years until it was possible. People seem to get this when it comes to physical rehabilitation, yet they have a harder time appreciating how difficult it is to reconstruct thoughts and alter behaviors in recovery from an eating disorder."

Another psychotherapist with a now-distant history of anorexia recalls the complexity of the challenge that restoration presented to her. "I never had a sense of self. I gauged my way of being in response to others, was always a reactor instead of an actor. My false self reigned while my real self quietly observed." That false self, whose name was ED, would not yield until the real self gathered enough strength, courage, and hope to reclaim her own life.

While quiet observation has its merits, your true self has the right to shout out loud. Restoration empowers you to assert that right, to come out of the shadows and step into your own spotlight, to begin making your own decisions and taking responsibility for your own choices while laying ED to rest. The idea is to nourish, nurture, and restore the person you were becoming when ED hijacked your identity.

This process will likely move forward in fits and starts. Occasional relapses are common in the early months and years of recovery. These do become milder and briefer as recovery progresses. Unfortunately, that's small consolation when you are going through a relapse. This poem, by college student Gillian Calig, who wrote her story alongside her mother's perspective in chapter 2, captures the painful messiness of this phase exquisitely.

MY SURRENDER

Nothing goes right
over and again.
You finally see the light
   And the ray is clouded over.
So much anxiety it is sickening.
You've fought, and fought
   Over and again.
I only have so much resilience,

I won't keep bouncing back
    I am no rubber ball.
My past may be promising,
    but my future is yet to be made.
Keep testing my strength,
    And I will break.
Sadly, yet happily,
    It will be welcomed.
Because there is no hope left in me
    and I have capitulated.

Gillian's poem reflects the feeling of failure that can rise up again and again during this phase. But for her, writing poetry offered one way to release that frustration. She's persevered, learning the patience "to enjoy the successes and be braced for the relapses," when and if they occur. Gillian is now riding these waves instead of getting sucked under by them.

Following treatment and weight stabilization, it's also common to enter what I call the half-life of eating disorders. Starving, bingeing, or purging are not the only ways to restrict, punish, or deny oneself. People caught in ED's half-life may push themselves on the job at the expense of sleep, relaxation, family, or friendships. Some compulsively shop, work out, or clean the house instead of admitting feelings of anger or sadness. Others deny themselves pleasure or intimacy, or turn to alcohol or drugs—all because of that familiar feeling of not being "good enough." These patterns have nothing to do with food or weight, but they're common extensions of eating disorders.

To live fully without ED, we have to restore *positive* passions that can gradually overtake the habit of suffering. The tricky part is that we all have different passions. One person may love horses. Another may love painting, or poetry. Still another may love teaching or raising children. Love is at the core of all passion. So restoring love to the everyday experience of life is a big part of recovery. But how can you tell what you love if you don't know who you are? This is the Trillion-Dollar Question for anyone returning to normal life after an eating disorder. And one way to answer it, at least initially, is through imitation.

We all are pros at imitation. As children we mimic the way our mothers exclaim when they answer the phone. Later, we modulate our voices to match our friends', or perhaps we adopt the lingo of admired colleagues at work. We copy recipes, accept book recommendations, borrow fashion ideas from television and magazines.

Imitation is hardwired into our brains from birth. Babies have to mirror those around them in order to learn how to speak, how to act, how to feel. This learning transpires through special neurons, logically called *mirror neurons,* which allow us not only to imitate the actions of others but also to share the emotions behind those actions. Thanks to mirror neurons, we both register and sense the pleasure of people we see smiling, the excitement of those we hear shouting, and the sadness of those we see crying. Mirror neurons, in other words, serve as our pathway to learning and empathy.

Scientists have found that mirror neurons remain active throughout life. After a traumatic injury or illness, such as an eating disorder, they can play a crucial role in the brain's fight back to normalcy. This happens when we consciously choose healthy examples to imitate.

I became keenly aware of this process as I recovered from anorexia in my twenties. After pushing away from friends and family for some seven years, I made a conscious decision to reach out to those who seemed to me most "normal." I watched the way my ebullient roommate ate and laughed. I studied the way classmates casually shared sandwiches and pizza while engrossed in talk about their futures. I imitated the way fearless friends seemed to seize opportunities and embrace adventures. When one of them applied to United Airlines to become a flight attendant, I followed her lead. When I fell in love, my husband prompted me to try foods such as knishes, calzones, margaritas, and Häagen-Dazs cakes—indulgences ED would have denied me.

I imitated my way back to a strong semblance of normalcy, and gradually I also came to feel more normal. My body looked hale. My eating habits seemed healthy. My spirits appeared secure. But imitation does have its limits. When I became anxious, I couldn't copy my way out of distress. No matter how cool and poised I might look to others, tension gnawed at my nerves. I could never fully measure up to the people I admired. Sooner or later someone was bound to find me out. How much of my life was I still faking? I didn't dare ask. Full recovery demanded that I move beyond imitation to restore my own true sense of self.

As the letters in this chapter make clear, this process of self-restoration is a complicated venture. Restoring one's true self means daring to look in the mirror and make peace with the imperfections, fears, and sorrows that stare back. It means trusting that person in the mirror to make authentic choices, fueled by desire rather than dread. Sometimes, as Merry discovered when she emerged from treatment at age fifty-one, that person can actively choose to *surrender* control:

> When trying to buy new clothes, such as a bathing suit, I use the employees of the store as fashion consultants. If I allow the fashion consultant to make the decision on which bathing suit or which size jeans look best on me, the control is taken out of my hands. I trust that person's choices and that takes away ED's criticism when looking in the mirror at home. I'm able to fan my nose at him. "Haha! I got you, ED. Go away!" Cutting out size tags that are stitched into the clothing is another step. Most of the time I can walk by a scale now without trying to measure my self-worth by jumping on it. My worth is not a math equation.

I love this note because it so beautifully illustrates the fallacy, which underscores every eating disorder, that control is a measure of personal character. The true measure of character is the ability to make healthy, compassionate, and constructive choices and to refuse destructive options. Having a strong sense of self does *not* mean being untouchable or flawless. On the contrary, it means that you appreciate both your vulnerabilities and your strengths, and that you're committed to learning how to balance them.

An eating disorder is not an identity; it's a pattern of thought and behavior that overwhelms your identity. This is why I hesitate to describe people as anorexics, bingers, or bulimics. The very language turns human beings into things, defined solely by their most disturbed behavior when, in fact, they're richly complex individuals with hearts, minds, and bodies that breathe with life. ED be damned, we all deserve to be treated by others, and especially by ourselves, with respect, honor, and appreciation.

This phase of restoration, then, is a time of active choices—to feel more alive than dead, to pursue dreams that are fulfilling rather than empty, to value experiences that are human rather than "perfect." These are the choices that culminate in the knowing and emphatic declaration of independence from ED.

Reagan: Passing the Shell

Now in her mid-twenties, Reagan is five years into recovery. She still finds it difficult at times to recognize the fine line that separates "disordered" from "recovered," but she's developed an impressive set of skills to ensure that she stays on the healthy side of that line.

FOR ME, THE BEGINNING of recovery was distinctly marked. My final group therapy session, the end of an extremely intensive outpatient schedule, included the ceremonial "passing of the shell." Group members both silently and aloud sent warm wishes and vibes into a seashell, which I got to keep as a source of comfort, hope, and remembrance for the journey that lay ahead. Additionally, I graduated from high school, marking a more physical departure from my old habits and patterns as I moved out of state to go to college.

Recovery was like setting off on a journey all its own. When I first began treatment, I'm sure that I viewed recovery as the end of everything. In both wonderful and terrible ways, it is just the beginning. To emphasize that it's truly an ongoing process and struggle, I insist on telling people that I'm "in recovery from an eating disorder" rather than "recovered from an eating disorder."

Recovery is an ever-changing animal that I experience in different ways on different days. Some days I'm overcome with a sense of gratitude and amazement that I actually lived through the emotional and physical traumas of anorexia. Other days, I long for the comfort of the illness that made it feel (falsely, of course) like everything could be fixed so easily and that achieving the perfect life was within my control. And other days, I feel that recovery is a grueling life sentence to which I've been condemned—always struggling, never succeeding. Make no mistake: recovery is an exhausting process.

I still have days when I waste an inordinate amount of energy relentlessly criticizing myself, and even though that worries my loved ones, recovery means that those days are fewer and farther between than before.

It is the good days and life-affirming moments that remind me why the struggle is worth it. When I dream about my future, when I laugh with my sister, when I kiss my true love, I know why I'm still here. Above all, I know that I must remain gentle with myself. I must forgive myself, honor my emotions, and allow room for change and growth. This is how I manage to stay on the "in recovery" side of that fine line.

I owe so much of my recovery to my treatment team (with whom I am still in touch), my family, and supportive friends. These people equipped me with a metaphorical toolbox: I have certain mantras to recite on hard days, funny quotes and memories to make me smile instantly, and a sense that I'm always part of a loving community that will accept me and guide me should I lose my way. And when recovery feels too hard or too overwhelming, I go to my bedside table, retrieve my seashell, and remember how far I've come.

Cheryl: My Body, My Friend

Cheryl suffered with her eating disorder for twenty-two years before she reached her turning point and committed herself to treatment, first in an inpatient, residential program, then in a day program, and finally an evening program. As an outpatient, she continued to work with a team that included two new therapists, a nutritionist, a primary-care MD, and a psychopharmacologist—all of whom specialized in eating disorders. They were ready to help her keep ED at bay. But what Cheryl discovered—and was able to accept only after graduating from treatment—was that her team was not ultimately responsible for her recovery. Rather, her continuing transformation depended on her treating herself with the same care, compassion, and wisdom that her therapists had shown her. She had to take charge of her own health, body and soul, using all the tools and lessons she'd learned.

INTRODUCING HEALTHY BEHAVIORS into my everyday life was challenging. When stresses came up in my workplace or in my home life, I wanted to run to ED. After all, for a lifetime that was my automatic. By pursuing healthy behaviors, I felt I was letting my best friend down.

However, recovery means pushing through the pain and engaging in health. I was able to utilize tools such as positive self-talk, talking back to ED. (ED was still loud, but I was talking back and telling him no. *I* was getting the last word. As my therapist, Thom Rutledge, told me, never let ED get the last word!), holding ice (instead of hurting myself when upset), chatting with friends, and journaling in order to interrupt ED's thoughts and behaviors.

Yoga and massage therapy remain essential practices in my life of recovery. I practice yoga twice a week and go for a massage every other week. They both help bring all my senses together to a place that finds acceptance.

Yoga teaches me how to relax and how to be in tune in mind and body. I learn how my body reacts to various poses and feel the strength it takes to hold my body in proper alignment. I disconnect my mind from daily stresses and any unhealthy thoughts and put forth a healthy vision. I begin to see and feel the real me.

Massage therapy brings me a sense of freedom . . . freedom from a negative body image and negative thoughts. I lie still, relaxed, with my eyes closed, and feel my body from the inside out, open to touch, a safe place where I do not judge myself. Massage therapy helps me see my body for the instrument and gift it is. It's not my enemy! When I leave that tranquil space, I'm ready to face the world with a sense of power, knowing that my mind and body are learning to become friends.

Sensing the Body
Why Mindfulness Practices Help
By Rachel M. Calogero

Mindfulness practices such as yoga and massage give us the means to experience our body and mind without judgment, to show ourselves respect and nurturance, and to exercise strength and fearlessness. Within these practices we sense our own truth—as Cheryl said, "the real me." Truth is liberating.

Mindfulness practices strengthen our connection to our genuine physical and emotional experiences, bypassing the repetitive, obsessive thought process of the eating disorder. Perhaps the defining quality of mindfulness practices is that they teach us to let go—to be present in the moment without holding on to the past or thinking about the future—by connecting more fully to our sense of self. In addition to yoga and massage, meditation, martial arts, a wide variety of body and breath work, voice and art therapy, and other expressive therapies can all help us to quiet our racing minds, garner and focus our energy, and connect to our bodies.

How does this promote recovery? The strong mind-body connection that mindfulness practices cultivate is ultimately incompatible with an eating disorder. By increasing self-awareness, focus, and self-acceptance, mindfulness helps you change negative behavior and thought patterns, make better choices, and be less reactive and less inclined to retreat to ED for comfort. While these practices do not get rid of fears and anxieties, they can reduce the grip of these emotions and help you move through them at your own pace to become more attuned to yourself.

Research has demonstrated that mindfulness practices also relieve a variety of conditions that often accompany eating disorders, such as depression and anxiety. By their very nature, mindfulness practices are not competitive, judgmental, or punishing. Instead, they teach us how to be compassionate, accepting, and forgiving of ourselves and our bodies. The goal of yoga, for example, is to foster a deep sense of meditative peace and relaxation. Meditation practices teach us to observe the quality of our everyday thoughts without judging them, to notice how they come and go—or sometimes stick like glue—but at the same time not get emotionally caught up in them. Through meditation training one can learn to let go of obsessive thinking and live out of a calmer center within oneself.

The experience of massage is more passive than some other mindfulness practices, yet it also encourages nonjudgmental thought and self-compassion. Through a variety of techniques, massage manipulates the soft tissue of the body, releasing stress and pent-up emotions. Massage therapy has been shown to improve mood and circulation and relieve tension and fatigue. Perhaps most important, the gentle and respectful touch of an experienced massage therapist gives us permission to be more gentle and nurturing with our own bodies.

Because eating disorders can be interwoven with depression, anxiety, shame, or traumatic memories that will naturally be encountered through mindfulness work, it's important to have the support and expertise of a trusted professional who is adept at guiding people through this process. When seeking the services of yoga, massage, and other mindfulness-practice teachers, always ask for reliable references, training, and certification.

Stella: Feel the Feeling

Stella began her recovery at forty-three, having struggled on and off with ED since she was fifteen. Born and raised in Brazil, she was married, had two healthy sons, and had seen several therapists throughout the years who helped her move toward recovery. Still, her bulimia had continued, intermittently at first, and had then eventually overwhelmed her. She felt herself to be an imposter in her own life because she could not control her illness. Only in recovery is she realizing that just the opposite is true.

THROUGHOUT THESE YEARS there were many things that seemed to work for a while, but they weren't enduring solutions because they used control to tame what supposedly was faulty behavior. Setting limits to food intake, setting rules, setting schedules—all of that needed to go at some point, because it related closely to self-doubt and my reluctance to rely on my body's signals and my feelings.

It's not about food, it's about my feelings. It's about my anger, my frustration, and my desire for big motherly arms to hold me and tell me that everything's all right and that I'm loved. It's about finally realizing that ED gave me something to hold when I was not allowed to have what I really needed.

The belief that it's all about my feelings has changed completely my way of dealing with myself. For the first time, I'm sure that I've found the right path.

Therapy has been an essential element, even when at times it seemed

I wasn't going anywhere. This perception, in fact, was still the judgmental one inside of me, which would measure growth by keeping tabs on bulimic episodes. But it's not about food. And when the truth of this statement hit me emotionally, that's when keeping tabs became a waste of time, or just one more control mechanism trying to keep me connected to old patterns.

It's a slow learning process, but awareness of the negative messages I send myself throughout the day is a good start. Connecting to my feelings of loneliness and letting my mind discover what my heart really needs has also been a great practice. I've been increasing this awareness daily in order to connect with the triggers before they can take hold of me. Sometimes it's just a quick flash, or a brief wave of fear and sadness. These are important signals.

Becoming an observer, without judgment, is complicated for those who are perfectionists by nature, but when there's doubt about what to do next, time can be a great ally. Wait . . . And if it is not clear yet, wait some more. This waiting, the practice of just being in the present, is at the heart of my recovery.

Stephanie: True Hunger

Stephanie, who in chapter 3 wrote about her difficulty reconciling her identity as an African-American woman with her eating disorder, agreed with Stella that her history of bulimia was rooted in feelings, not food. But she also found that something wonderful happened when she learned to separate the two—she learned to feel and appreciate hunger!

TODAY MY RELATIONSHIP with food has healed. I've learned the difference between real physical hunger and emotional eating.

For a long time in my early recovery I had no connection to my body's natural cues. I simply thought I was hungry all the time. Morning, noon, and night I felt a hunger for food, something to fill me up and replace whatever was missing. Through therapy I learned to distinguish between eating to elevate my mood and eating to sustain my body. If I'm stressed or tired, lonely or angry, my body immediately signals for more food. Before I take that first bite now, I'm able to stop and ask, "What or who am I wanting to eat over?" It could mean that someone or something triggered my shame button. Usually, but not always, the answer comes quickly.

I've accepted that hunger is a yardstick I can use to measure my emotional life. Now I get to deal with the real reasons I wanted to eat.

Bridget: Out of Poverty

The reasons behind Bridget's eleven-year battle with ED were economic as well as emotional. Now a twenty-four-year-old student supporting herself as a nanny, she understands that restoring her physical health is a basic requirement for establishing her financial health. But the mythology that surrounds eating disorders once led her to think just the opposite.

JUST TWO MONTHS AGO I was asked to be the guest speaker at a local conference on eating disorders as a story of hope. If someone had told me five years ago that I'd be sharing my *positive* journey in front of an audience, I'd have rolled my eyes. At that time I *was* my eating disorder—and I was proud of it. So much has happened since then . . .

Growing up, I was embarrassed by my family's poverty and by all of the fighting that went on in my house. I had so many secrets. As the oldest of four, I thought I had to take care of the finances, since my parents couldn't. By the time I was sixteen, I'd opened a checking account and was writing bad checks because my parents told me it was the only way we'd be able to eat, have electricity, or pay any other bills. They were correct, but it was a lot to handle at that age! I was also taking care of them emotionally by constantly trying to solve their problems as well as keep our financial status a secret in our very small town. That pressure was one of the reasons I tried to numb myself by not eating. It was too much for me to support the adults in my life.

People say (and write!) that eating disorders tend to occur only in upper-class females. I met a wealthy girl in treatment once who told me I couldn't have a real eating disorder because I didn't go to a tough private school and because I was from a rural area where I could never feel the same pressures as she did. Really! The truth is, I had the same influence of the media and peer pressure to look like my friends (more pressure, since I couldn't afford the trendy clothes), plus poverty pushed me to do well in school so that one day I could get out of my home situation. Social and financial status has no bearing on the way someone feels or deals with those feelings.

When I developed my eating disorder around the age of twelve, I thought that if I could lose a few pounds, people would like me more. Maybe someone would care about me. Hey, I might even find somebody to love me when I felt like my parents didn't (they were each struggling with their own demons).

Only in treatment was I able to open up a little. Here and there in group therapy or in a private session I'd tiptoe out of my usual mute state and toss tiny bits of information into the air, each one like a hundred-pound weight off my shoulders. Each time I relapsed, I'd go back to treatment and open up a little more, until finally I was able to trust, share, and give recovery a fair shot. It took five years, and I said "I quit!" almost constantly, but once I was able to break through the shame and silence of my past, I found that others liked who I was, not because I was sick or thin but just because I was me. Once I was able to see that, I began to feel more comfortable opening up to people outside of treatment and making connections in the real world.

I can't keep secrets any longer. I really believe that you're only as sick as your secrets. When I'm unable to be myself and tell my truth, I'm still holding on to sickness. I can't keep my parents' secrets any longer, either. Nor can I rescue them by ignoring my own needs and giving away what I've worked for.

My parents are still struggling financially, but I've realized (with a lot of help) that I cannot support them economically any longer. I've come to terms with the fact that helping my parents ruined my credit and that it's not my job to take care of them. When I give all that I have to them, I leave nothing for myself and am left worn out and empty.

Recovery reminds me of the instruction flight attendants give on an airplane, to put your own oxygen mask on first before you try to help others. I still feel guilty sometimes knowing that my parents are not making good financial choices with the little money they do have, but I also realize that I am a graduate student without much money myself, and when I don't take care of myself on the little money that I earn as a nanny, I'm unable to take care of anyone else. Then I'll never break the cycle of poverty.

I also know that I'll never get that MSW I'm working toward nor will I succeed in a job and live a financially stable life if I don't eat properly. There are just so many reasons to be healthy!

Leila: *I* Am *Worthy*

Now thirty-eight, Leila has been wrestling with bulimia for twenty years. She began treatment at twenty-four, combining one-on-one counseling with group therapy and nutritional education, but it wasn't until she went through an intensive, fifteen-week recovery program at age thirty-three that she dared to consider herself recovered. The program shifted her focus from weight- and food-related issues to the broader task of building a meaningful life. Paradoxically, it was a relapse about a year later that finally revealed the real reasons why she let ED gain power over her—and what she needed to do to fully regain her freedom.

WHEN I FOUND MYSELF in a personal crisis, ED presented itself as an ally, and I grasped it like a life preserver. I welcomed the symptoms, which had mutated from the usual binge/purge cycle to more anorexic-like qualities. I felt safe and in control even as important relationships crumbled around me.

Through this relapse, I came to face the reality that ED is a default response to anxiety in my life and therefore I have to be ever-vigilant, consciously choosing other means for self-calming when varying levels of stress present themselves.

What helps me feel most engaged and alive day to day? I have to say that this question is itself, in a way, the answer: when I'm fully engaged in life (that is, honestly self-aware), I feel most alive. It's vital for me to be in the moment, regardless of whether that's a pleasant or an unpleasant place to be. Feelings of anxiety, loneliness, sadness, and boredom are uncomfortable feelings, but like other aspects of life, even these unpleasant emotions are fluid and will therefore pass.

To be present, it's necessary to acknowledge my feelings as soon as I become aware of them. By so doing, I'm able to accept them and remind myself that they will pass and that I'll feel OK again without using unhealthy means to suppress or avoid the feelings.

It's essential to recognize that I have needs and to express those needs to myself as well as to the important people in my life. It sends a message to my brain that I am worthy and valuable.

I visualize the thought patterns that lead me to ED as well-worn tracks in my brain. I just need to get my thoughts to jump off those tracks and onto a healthier line of thinking in order to avoid the train wreck of binge-ing and purging.

I function so much better when I treat myself in the way that I like to be treated by others: nonjudgmentally and with the utmost gentle-ness. Whenever I was feeling low in the past, I'd be self-critical. Now I've learned to become my own best friend and take steps to treat myself even more lovingly.

Practicing yoga challenges my body in a gentle and loving way and has taught me to appreciate its abilities. Needlework is my passion, and the repetitive nature of drawing thread through fabric transports my mind into a near-meditative state. Writing to my best friend as though I'm actually sitting across from her allows me to access and release my true feelings. The honest sharing of feelings is like a detoxification of pent-up negative emotions.

COPING MECHANISMS
Tips for Stress Management
By Angela Favaro

We normally feel stress in situations we think we can't handle. When the threat is physical, stress functions like an alarm to get the whole body into life-preserving fight-or-flight mode. But often the degree of stress we experience depends on how we view the conflict, and on the resources we have to cope with it. With the right coping skills at the ready, we can feel calmer even when facing circumstances that otherwise would cause distress.

Improving your ability to manage stress starts with three basic guidelines:

1. *Understand that stress is normal.* To be under stress or to feel stressed does not mean you're disabled, weak, or incompetent. Stress is simply a signal that can help you recognize your needs. Criticizing yourself for feeling stressed or trying to suppress the feeling will only increase your anxiety and make it *more* difficult to handle the situation. Acknowledging the feeling of stress is the first step toward successfully managing it.

2. *Take stock of your current stress-management resources and abilities.* The more resources you have to help you manage the stressful situation, and the stronger your coping strategies, the less stress you'll feel. Identify the resources and relationships in your life that currently help you manage stress (for example, people you know you can turn to for help or support, a beloved pet, a favorite hobby) as well as the factors that limit your ability to manage stress (such as fatigue, lack of free time, unsupportive relationships).

3. *Identify the resources and abilities you still need to develop in order to succeed in managing stress.* Make a list of new practices, friendships, and experiences you'd like to cultivate to help you feel more in balance and better able to manage stress. For example, proven stress-management practices include meditation, relaxing in nature, dedicating time to hobbies and sports, and socializing with close friends. Write out small steps you can take to incorporate these elements into your life on a regular basis. Then make sure to take one of these steps every day. Effective stress management is not a quick fix but a lifelong process.

Because eating disorders themselves often begin as desperate, if counterproductive, efforts to manage stress, it's important during recovery to review what was happening in your life at the time your ED began. Turning to food, restricting food intake, and fixating on weight and body shape can be an attempt to escape or overcome emotions or situations that feel overwhelming. What were those feelings? What were the situations that caused them? The longer you've had an ED, the more difficult it may be to push through the preoccupation with food and weight to examine the conflicts that lie underneath, but as you develop healthier and more effective coping skills, it will feel safer to examine those original sources of stress. And as you gain perspective on those conflicts, you'll build confidence in your ability to overcome them.

During recovery, it's especially important to remember that most people either eat too much or lose their appetite during times of stress. But for months or even years after an eating disorder, your body may remain acutely sensitive to changes in weight or food intake. Appetite fluctuations that others would take in stride may intensify your feelings of stress, leading to further changes in your eating and/or weight and possible relapse. So pay attention to any changes in your appetite, as well as to other physical warning signals, such as sleeplessness or fatigue, and look for sources of stress in your life that may be causing the change. Rather than focusing on food and weight, concentrate on resolving these conflicts and managing stress through healthy coping skills.

As you take good care of your body, it will teach you when something is awry and what you need to feel strong and healthy. The best stress-management resource of all is a lifestyle that respects your own emotional, physical, and spiritual needs.

Halley: The Long View

Halley was thirty-four years old and five months into recovery when she first wrote to me. She'd battled bulimia for about sixteen years and couldn't figure out how to let it go. She'd been in therapy and read numerous books on recovery, yet periods of severe stress or anxiety always sent her back to ED. A vicious cycle began, as shame over "failing" to stop made her ever more secretive in her bingeing and purging. Then one day, everything changed.

THE CATALYST WAS a confrontation with my husband. He called me out on evidence that I was again bingeing and purging. For years he'd pleaded with me to understand how crucial it was for me to stop this behavior, how damaging it was to my health, my teeth, my body, and (during my pregnancies) to our children. That night he asked if I'd been bingeing and purging again, and I told him I hadn't. He didn't believe me. He was so angry, he said he was finished. He wanted no part in our marriage, in my continual lies or my unwillingness to take responsibility for my disorder.

So there I was, alone. That's the number-one thing you get from bulimia: you pull away from everyone important. I'd reached the lowest point in my life.

I turned to God. After identifying the things that seemed to incapacitate me and make me feel overwhelmed, I made the choice to give them to God. Knowing that he knows how to navigate me through these burdens allows me to give up the control that I'm desperately trying to hold on to. At the same time, *I have the power to walk away from bulimia by trusting myself to be responsible.*

Mary Anne Cohen's book, *French Toast for Breakfast,* helped me identify whether I was eating because of physical hunger or emotional hunger. When it's emotional hunger, I need to figure out what's bothering me and deal with it instead of escaping or hiding from it.

One of the tools I've found helpful is to keep a daily food journal. Each day I write down all the food I've eaten. I also record when I'm feeling particularly sad, down, and so on. This helps me see if I'm overeating or restricting my food intake during these times. I won't binge and purge. Sure, I know I can, but I choose to hold myself accountable.

I've found healthier and more productive ways to calm down and think things through. One that tops the list is praying (to actually talk out loud and have a conversation with God—cry, yell, laugh, discuss). It's also been very helpful to reveal to close friends and relatives that I'm bulimic, and to write down my thoughts, fears, frustrations, and my personal story with bulimia.

I've also been attending a monthly eating-disorders support group sponsored by my church. To know you're not alone, to identify with others going through some of the same issues as you—it feels good to talk about it and get it out! And it feels good to listen, too. This has brought my eating disorder out of isolation—and isolation is where bulimia thrives.

Now that I'm no longer using bulimia to cope, I see (very clearly and painfully) the mess I've made of my life and my relationships. The empowering thing is that I finally realize I have an impact on my life and the choices I make, and that I must deal with the consequences instead of hiding or trying to escape from them.

My children help me see joy that's innocent and simple. Every day I get to spend with them makes me realize that I have two wonderful reasons to be and stay healthy. Some of the fun things we do together are chasing one another around the house, making silly faces, singing really loudly in the car, reading books together, exploring outside. They are such perfect little people.

I can either hinder or encourage my children by the ways I engage with them, accept them, and help them come into their own. I want more than anything to be a strong, positive, helpful role model for them, to help them grow and mature and become responsible people, to encourage them to do things by themselves and not be scared to try new things. This is where my focus should be.

My recovery has also helped me realize so many ways I isolated my husband from the inner me. I was ashamed of what he'd see, but the more isolated I became, the more our marriage was being torn down. I was so naive to think that ED affected only me.

Several months later, Halley wrote with a bad-news/good-news update.

I FOUND OUT that my husband has been having an affair with a coworker since the time he told me he was done with my eating disorder and done with our marriage. I'm currently in the final stages of finalizing the divorce.

It's been a very difficult emotional roller coaster for me the last several months, but I'm so very proud and happy to tell you that I have remained binge/purge-free. I've continued to attend my monthly support group and have been seeing a therapist who specializes in eating disorders and in marriage and family therapy. These two things, in addition to my family and friends, have really been a huge source of support.

Through it all I've continued to keep God in my daily thoughts and choices. God has not let go of me. He's shown me how to deal and cope with extremely emotional and difficult feelings in a new, healthier way, and he's continued to teach me how to trust and value myself and my feelings.

RECOVERY AND RELIGION
The Role of Spirituality in Recovery

By John F. Morgan

It's natural when emerging from an eating disorder to wonder, "What is my purpose?" "What's the meaning of my life?" "What do I believe in?" That's because chronic illness often becomes entangled with the search for meaning. When we experience emotional and physical suffering, we tend to look inward for sources of motivation, comfort, and encouragement to get us through. ED can distort spiritual beliefs and practices, making them part of the illness. Low self-esteem and a self-critical or self-punitive attitude can fuel a belief in a critical, judgmental, or punitive God, higher being, or universal energy. Virtue and self-worth become equated with abstinence and self-denial. Reversing these distortions of faith and value, then, is vital for the full restoration of health.

As you recover, you may find yourself questioning your most fundamental beliefs about who you are. Sometimes this line of existential questioning will lead you to reexamine your spiritual beliefs or reconsider the role of spirituality in your life. Though unsettling at first, this process ultimately can be deeply rewarding.

Full and frank exploration of your spiritual beliefs and values with a trusted advisor can reinforce a positive sense of yourself and your purpose, and help motivate you to nurture and nourish yourself, body and soul. Your minister, rabbi, chaplain, or other religious advisor can help you distinguish your genuine and affirming spiritual beliefs and practices from those connected to the eating disorder. So can your therapist.

It's not necessary for you and your therapist to share a religious or spiritual orientation in order to explore together this aspect of your life. We all contend with questions about happiness and what makes a good life. It's sufficient simply for your therapist to be open, willing, and able to ask the relevant questions that can help you sort through your own values and beliefs.

Treatment that's person-centered and holistic will naturally include an awareness and acknowledgment of the spiritual dimension of life. Mindfulness is one specific, nondenominational practice frequently used in clinical treatment to promote self-awareness and heightened focus. The practice of mindfulness helps to quiet your body and mind, and more fully experience your consciousness and true perceptions. This can increase your sense of wonder at the world, and deepen your quest for meaning.

Exploring your spirituality through mindfulness and honest discussions with a trusted therapist or advisor, and through your own questioning and personal observation, can open doors to new levels of hope, inspiration, and possibility as you return fully to life.

Laura: The Whole Truth

Laura had endured her eating disorder for decades when she discovered she could talk to herself in a voice that did not belong to ED. Unlike the harsh, shaming, tyrannical diatribe she was used to, this new self-talk was more compassionate, vulnerable, and forgiving. The surprise for Laura as she wrote about this transformation four years later was that this softer voice opened up so many different aspects of her life.

IT'S NOW OBVIOUS TO ME that what brings people together is not their perfection but their imperfections. We all want to be loved and supported, but we also want to be given the opportunity to give love and support. It's extremely helpful to remind myself of this during my down moments. Being open and honest about my struggles and insecurities makes me more at ease in anxious situations. By voicing my weaknesses I'm able to establish real honest connections with people based on love, trust, and teamwork. I'm discovering the pleasure of shedding expectations of myself.

Recovery is a journey with many stops and setbacks, periods of enlightenment, hope, and motivation, and moments of helplessness and nostalgia. I've learned to sit through these, to build my confidence, stop taking ED so seriously, and even talk back.

Through yoga I try to make peace with my body and at some moments can even feel grateful for what my body can do. Music with meaningful lyrics and empowering tunes gets me out of my little world and puts things into perspective. And I've recently taken up hand drumming. It's amazing how generating a simple rhythm can feel so satisfying.

Michele: Walking Tall

Among those who understand eating disorders, recovery means feeling good and maintaining good health at any size. Unfortunately, misconceptions about the meaning of weight persist in the rest of our culture. This can be especially hurtful to those in recovery whose weight is high. Michele had struggled with Binge Eating Disorder for most of her forty-nine years, regardless of her size. She found it difficult to get appropriate care because of the common misperception that healthy weight and eating behavior are governed by willpower and/or the right diet. Today she's divorced, works as an information-technology manager, and is considering graduate school. Her health is good and her spirit strong, but she must still overcome daily challenges to her self-confidence.

IN MY GRASS-IS-ALWAYS-GREENER MIND, it would be far easier to have bulimia or anorexia because people seem to understand those problems more clearly. Also, when you have those disorders, you aren't still fat after weight-loss surgery—chances are, whatever's wrong with you is exceedingly more acceptable than being fat.

Is it that people are offended by the idea that we fat girls erect our own barrier to keep people away? Maybe I'm giving people too much credit, but that's more comforting than the alternative.

Today, my doctor gently tells me that all my gynecological problems would be solved by losing weight.

I make a point of asking, "What happens when skinny women get these problems?"

He tells me that with them it's an incurable cancer; when fat girls get these problems, it's an annoying but curable cancer and many times not even that.

When I tell my doc I've lost fifty pounds, he suggests maybe the hospital weight-loss program would help me lose the rest.

I tell him I've been through that program.

He retorts, "If you have this all figured out, why haven't you lost more weight?"

This kind of day is a smack in the face. My doctor can still make me cry. A forty-minute sit in the parking lot is how long it takes to recover.

Unfortunately, I still believe I need my fat to protect me. But I trust myself to find my own path now, crooked and jagged as it may be. When I put on bright clean expensive exercise shoes, with my iPod and sport earphones, I become an athlete walking in the park, and the panicked feeling of being dead is gone. When my hands are writing or sewing, they're not free to hold food. It's difficult to hold a melty chocolate bar while turning the pages of a book. A needle and thread, bottle of glue, brush full of paint, screws and screwdriver keep fingers from holding a spoon and a pint of Häagen-Dazs.

I'm still alive, and I can find evidence of that on a daily basis. I know this job will always be with me to a greater or lesser degree, but if I can collect more of my at-the-park walking moments and less of those fat-girl doctor's-office appointments, it may all work out for the best.

TRUTH TELLING
Five Challenges in Recovery from Binge Eating Disorder
By Amy Pershing

In my clinical practice working with individuals with binge eating disorder, I've observed five key challenges that people meet on the road to recovery. Some affect only those at high body weight. Most are related to issues that arise with all eating disorders. But in their subtleties these hurdles are unique to recovery from binge eating disorder.

1. Listening to Yourself

Michele says that recovery, for her, means that "the panicked feeling of being dead is gone." Many of my clients learned long ago to deaden feelings, sensations, and needs. They've kept family secrets or hidden trauma and abuse. They've been caregivers, protectors of siblings or parents, "adults" in the bodies of children. Perhaps the most significant moment in recovery from binge eating disorder is the individual's recognition that there is a true self inside, underneath ED's ever-persuasive voice. Recovery begins to take hold as the individual learns to listen to what may at first be only fleeting authentic experiences of emotions, sensations, thoughts, and needs.

2. Feeling Your Emotions

I've worked with many binge eaters who are profoundly emotionally perceptive. Food, often early in their lives, became a refuge from overwhelming emotions, a substance to comfort the self and numb feelings the child could not understand. Recovery, then, means letting go of this need to numb, learning to feel and manage powerful emotions, and developing the skills to understand and cope with strong feelings.

3. Expressing Your Truth

The body can be a powerful symbol, a truth teller, for those with binge eating disorder. Many of my clients fear that losing weight will mean losing their story—akin to disappearing without a trace. When they learn other healthy ways to express the truth of their lives—with words, with sound, with art—they no longer need to use their body size to tell the tale.

4. Honoring Your Body

Those who suffer from binge eating disorder have learned, with the aid of a culture that promotes reliance on diet and beauty gurus and a fundamental distrust of natural appetites, to ignore their body's needs and signals. A critical challenge in recovery is to recognize and become responsive to the body's language. This entails making decisions about what to eat, and when to stop, based on body wisdom rather than diet mythology.

5. Owning Your Own Recovery

The diet and beauty industries often define successful recovery by pounds shed. Even well-intentioned physicians such as Michele's often shame people into losing weight in order to conform to weight or BMI charts that aren't actually correlated to any true measure of longevity. It's imperative that individuals learn to define recovery for themselves and own their unique path to recovery.

Kimberly: The Resilient Self

Now thirty, Kimberly had been wrestling with her eating disorder for seventeen years when she finally entered a residential treatment program. She wrote a few months after treatment, pointing out that the precariousness of this stage of recovery has a lot to do with other people's misperceptions of eating disorders. To get better, you have to build up resilience not only to the cultural forces that promote eating disorders but also to the stigma that surrounds them.

I'M A FEW MONTHS into recovery (for the second time), and there's such a vast contrast between my protected (and somewhat fragile) world and the "real" world right now. I know other girls (and guys) struggling with recovery feel it too—the "Aren't you better yet?" Or the assumption that you *are* all better and therefore should be back to work/school, back to life as it was (or appeared to be to them) before. As if inpatient treatment were some magic method guaranteed to heal you, whether or not insurance permitted you to receive an adequate amount of treatment.

Oddly, something I wrote years ago about grieving applies to this aspect of recovery—as if ED were a loved one who's just died but still dominates your life: "You feel compelled to play or resume the role of the same persevering lady, dynamic yet sincere friend, loyal sister, dedicated (and bright) student, loving daughter. But then one day you look around and see that everyone believes this façade you've put up (and that you almost believe it yourself); everyone forgets so quickly what just happened in your life. They once again get too wrapped up in what's going on in their lives to remember the great loss you just incurred in yours. And you feel lost and alone, just going through the motions of everyday life, but you don't show it . . . ."

People don't get that you're challenged by things that aren't even an issue for them. Getting dressed in regular clothes or being out and about downtown on Saturday night, even if you just to go out to eat, represents a huge deal, a triumph.

Last night I was trying to express my anger and frustration with the stigmas of society, stigmas that I find myself having already bought into or still buy into, even when I'm working so hard to reject them. I know it will always be a slippery slope. Beauty products that tell us we're not firm, smooth, thin, or good enough can easily give way to the rationale that we're just pampering ourselves, giving ourselves an advantage, a little help, which can turn into just wanting to keep up with everyone else who's looking younger and younger even as they age. Suddenly you find yourself wanting more and more of society's ideals of beauty, and without even realizing it, the negative self-talk becomes normal. It's a slippery slope, or more like those amusement-park rides where, strapped in a mile high up, you're dropped over the edge.

Society's messages and increasingly unrealistic ideals are so pervasive, it's maddening. You're trying to fight ED, fight for self-acceptance, fight to believe in your self-worth in a world that tells you the opposite everywhere you look. It's like trying to fight your way through a bustling crowd going the opposite way. Every time you move toward the goal (or even when you don't), you're being hit, pushed, bumped. Even if I fight not to buy into these messages, I'm inundated with them and surrounded by people who have bought into them.

But the stronger I get, I know the less they'll affect me. It's exhausting to try to justify the importance, severity, and magnitude of eating disorders to friends, family, lawyers, employers, magazines, the media, and even medical professionals—pretty much everyone, but it is more than worth it. I hope one day we'll have a louder voice (I'm still struggling to find mine) in order to fight for those who are suffering, to fight publicly, without shame or embarrassment, for their right to full treatment.

Tina: The Best of Friends

In chapter 3 Tina described the benefit she'd experienced working with a therapist who herself had a history of eating disorders. Here Tina reflects on the pleasures of life three years into recovery.

ONE OF THE MOST VITAL LESSONS I've learned is how I consistently validated negative feelings about myself, not only through my eating disorder but in other aspects of my life, including relationships. I'd been so good in setting boundaries, yet allowed in individuals who reconfirmed the negative feelings I had about myself: *You are not good enough!*

In particular, I dated a young man for the duration of my eating disorder, and the relationship shared many of the characteristics of my anorexia: emotionally draining, self-punishing, and lonely. When he confessed to being unfaithful for the second time because he "needed an emotionally stronger woman who wasn't so governed by her feelings," I wasn't that surprised.

But while I could have retreated back into ED's self-destructive and unhealthy patterns, I instead drew on the energy of my recovery. I let the social support of family and friends remind me that if I'd overcome an eating disorder, any subsequent life events were manageable.

Now I'm diligent about scheduling dinner dates, experimenting with new restaurants and cuisines. It's more than the food—it's the times spent with friends and family, making the memories that were absent from my life with an eating disorder.

Through recovery, I gained a deeper appreciation for simplicity. I relish now moments like my first sip of morning coffee, or a walk in the fresh air. I take naps now and honor my body when I feel tired. I've learned to be more gentle and patient with myself, as I am with others.

Leigha and Brad: Restoring Love

Leigha and Brad, the young couple who wrote as a duet in chapter 2, are now well into the restoration phase of Leigha's recovery and

stronger than ever as a result of fighting ED together. Neither pre-
tends that the fight is over or that life is perfect, but both agree that
meeting the challenge together has restored their marriage.

Leigha

IT'S NOW BEEN A YEAR AND A HALF since my last therapy session, and three years since I first sought help, and I'm proud to say I am still in recovery. My husband has been a true partner, and I attribute much of the success I've had to the support he's so lovingly provided me.

I'm still not sure if full recovery is possible. I still have to deal with lingering family issues that continue to spur old feelings of loss of control. I still have a tendency to feel like controlling my food will make everything better. However, I've learned to create much healthier coping mechanisms: exercise, journaling, reading a book, sharing the situation with my husband. Now that I have the tools to get me through the bad days, I feel I can grow.

Recovery at this point means the opportunity to experience love, happiness, and freedom. Unchaining myself from the numbers game of counting calories and from the habit of measuring my happiness by my weight or the size of my pants is such a liberating feeling. The freedom to not obsess over what others think of me and to just be happy with who I am would be the most freeing feeling of all.

Brad

TODAY MY WIFE CONTROLS HER FUTURE and is no longer a prisoner to the weight on the scale or the calories consumed the previous day. She's achieved levels of personal and professional success that could never have been achieved with her old mind-set. She looks forward to the surprises that come with waking up and not knowing what wonderful experiences she may encounter that day. She realizes that everyone has bad days and that that's OK.

Life isn't perfect; certain family members do still trigger old feelings and temporarily entice her to revert to old habits. However, today we're able to recognize these events, discuss the associated emotions, and move past them. I'm not sure these triggers will ever go away, but we avoid dangerous situations and deal with any bumps in the road. We're both better individuals, and stronger, for having dealt with this eating disorder together.

A Friend in Deed
Building Healthy Relationships

By Mary Tantillo

Humans thrive in connection to each other; we all need healthy and true friendships. But ED may have sabotaged your relationships by pretending to be your best friend and discouraging you from trusting or perhaps even approaching others who might support you. In fact, ED acts as an agent of disconnection and isolation, playing off your insecurities about appearance, popularity, identity, and uncertainty, as well as deeper anxieties. This not only deters you from developing healthy friendships, but may also nudge you toward negative relationships that end up promoting illness.

The first step toward building healthier relationships is to name the ways that ED controls your current friendships. For example, do you hear ED's voice:

- Telling you the other person will never like you?
- Warning that you're not thin enough or attractive enough to be seen with your friend?
- Insisting that, regardless of how you look, you're not good enough and therefore don't deserve to be that person's friend?
- Whispering that others can't be trusted to truly understand your experiences, and that they'll inevitably hurt you?

Make a list of the negative messages ED tells you, and share them with your therapist or another trusted mentor—someone who'll encourage you to make new friends in spite of ED's distortions.

The second step is to learn what a healthy friendship looks and feels like. A true mutual relationship gives both people an increased sense of self-worth, empowerment, zest or energy, clarity about themselves and each other, and desire for more connection with others. In genuine friendships, it's OK to show each other your emotional vulnerabilities because that helps you open up and feel empathy for each other. By sharing your thoughts, feelings, and needs you can help each other see how these perceptions influence you, and whether or not they're accurate. And when genuine friends disagree, they're willing to work to repair any damage, listening to one another and taking responsibility for their own part in the problem.

When choosing your friends, look for people who:

- Accept the whole of who you are—including both your strengths and limitations
- Enjoy the ways you're both similar, but also respect and appreciate your differences
- Are able and willing to help when you're in trouble
- Support your recovery by encouraging you to stay aware of your own thoughts, needs, and feelings while also considering those of others
- Gently help you look at problems from all sides
- Encourage you to discuss your concerns with others and have other friendships

As you seek and make true friends, expect ED to attempt to deplete and derail you in order to maintain its own relationship with you—and remember that this is a cardinal sign of an unhealthy friend. Try to ride out your fear of rejection, and consider talking to your friends about your anxieties. If you aren't comfortable doing that yet, then write them down and discuss them first with your therapist or a trusted mentor. By checking out your thoughts and feelings, you'll become more self-aware and learn to be a healthier friend to yourself. And that will enable you to dismiss ED's lies as you build the healthy relationships you genuinely deserve.

Ela: A Sense of Meaning

Ela's unique journey in healing involves travel, concerns about the environment, growing food, and sustainability—and highlights the critical and complicated role that a sense of purpose plays in recovery. Ela suffered from anorexia throughout her teens and early twenties, but she refused medical treatment. She got married, moved to the United States from the United Kingdom, and entered a PhD program in Classical Literature. Then, seven years ago, when she was twenty-five, her marriage ended. Suddenly her illness took over her life, and she spent three months in the hospital. After her release she again refused medical care, instead working with a meditation therapist. As she gained strength, she spent most of her free time outdoors, volunteering at the community garden, trying to "get grounded." But it would take another two years before she felt fully restored.

Unfortunately, dogma can easily be mistaken for purpose, and during recovery many individuals substitute righteous rules, especially around food and exercise, for the righteous restriction of the eating disorder. The challenge, as Ela so eloquently describes, is to separate judgmental patterns that limit the quality of life from truly healthy practices that open up and add genuine purpose to life.

SOMETHING I HEARD myself say at a group session in hospital, when I could barely formulate a thought, was, "What's wrong with me is that I've become disconnected from the flow of love." At the time, this barely made sense to me. In retrospect, however, this insight has informed all the quests and relocations of my post-nadir life: I've been searching for integration, for a sense of groundedness, connection, and meaning in life.

I've spent most of my time working on reintegration in different ways: volunteering for community-garden and community fruit-harvest projects, running potlucks, helping run the kitchen at retreats, learning massage, learning to be a beekeeper and tree worker. I felt passionate about all this hard and generally unpaid work, and that saw me move around in the Bay Area, and then to Hawaii's Big Island, where I lived on several farms at different times. It's all been beneficial in that it forced me to maintain my physical strength and would not permit me to starve myself. But early in recovery I pursued a largely vegan diet, and believed myself recovered, righteous, and healthy. In retrospect, I was very weak, nervous, low in stamina, and very often hungry. I was riddled with food taboos and rituals, still worrying a lot about whether I'd eaten too much.

Food and its preparation has been a preoccupation of mine my whole life. I was raised in an atmosphere in which there were definite judgments about which foods were good and which were not, as well as judgments about people based on what and how much they ate.

While it was wonderful to learn so much about fruits and vegetables and to harvest locally so much of what I ate, part of my motivation was extreme frugality. My interest in conservation of the environment and natural resources was intermeshed with a lesson I'd internalized in grade school: that taking care of myself was depriving someone else. When I harvested, I generally took for myself only what was spoiled or old. The bargain-produce shelf at the grocery store was the only shelf I'd allow myself to buy from. The strawberries at the farmer's market seemed too expensive, so I'd hang around and pick up the ones that fell on the street. It felt like the only food that appealed to me was what nobody else wanted, so I could be sure I wasn't depriving anyone else. These practices were probably as detrimental to my gut flora as my self-worth. I note that I'm still attracted to food that's being thrown out or discarded on the ground, but I've been working to retrain myself!

In Hawaii I met my husband, then moved with him to Alaska. Although he's almost twice my age, he is an incredible athlete and explorer, busy and unremittingly active almost every moment. I plunged into his vigorous, erratic, outdoors, hunting-fishing-hiking-camping lifestyle. Between trying to keep up with him and my propensity to diet, as well as some undiagnosed medical problems, I burned out my body again.

The whole time, I refused medical intervention. So although connection to the earth has been a constant for me, genuine integration remained elusive. Only in recent months have I finally begun to identify and medically address some of the long-term damage, and to surrender to my body's insistence on more consistency and less impulsive behavior (especially in response to someone else's!). At the start of my recovery, I couldn't even feel how constantly starving-hungry I was, still less intuit what my body needed when. And the whole time I've been "in recovery," up till recently, my diet was based on external dogmas, whether nutritional or environmental.

Now, in an Alaskan winter, it would be beyond my ingenuity to force myself to eat only locally harvested foods. I finally am eating what I need rather than what I think I should be eating.

Although the Hydra of anorexia keeps growing new heads, I'm feeling somewhat hopeful about my current trend toward self-acceptance, avoidance of dogma-based eating, and acquisition of a new sense of meaning. The blessing emerging from this return to physical weakness is that it's given me space to return to my writing, which is the one consistent presence in this overly erratic life path.

I'm tentatively finding joy and meaning in the identification of myself as a writer, and hoping that through the commitment to pursue this, instead of trying to live up to other people's standards, I'll finally be able to find some sense of meaning and connection.

Angela: All the Right Reasons

Angela is a mother of three who wrote about setting the stage for her recovery in chapter 2. Two years ago she went through a divorce. The following year, she went through a residential treatment program for her eating disorder. Now thirty-nine, she wrote this letter on the first anniversary of her recovery.

MORE IMPORTANT THAN accepting the weight, I've learned that nothing will make my life perfect. Wearing a size 2, for me, means being weak, sick, and unable to take care of my children. It means not having a period, not having a personality, being tired all the time, never laughing or smiling. It didn't solve my problems—in fact it led to the demise of my marriage.

I'm moving away from my meal plan toward Intuitive Eating now, a decision supported by my dietitian. I take my medication every day without fail. I get outside for some form of physical exercise daily, for my depression and stress relief, but I don't freak out anymore if I miss a day.

I wear a size that Mother Nature intended for me. My dietitian told me on my last appointment that my weight may go up again before stabilizing as my body adjusts to having a monthly cycle again. I'm glad she told me not to freak out, because I think that's happening now.

I know now that true happiness does not lie in the size or shape of my body. It lies in being able to laugh again, in being able to like myself, in recognizing that my authentic self is back, finally, after all these years. It lies in spending time with my children, enjoying them for today—and not spending my time with them thinking about what I ate or what I want to eat or what I shouldn't have eaten.

I'm once again the Angela I was born to be, the Angela that I remember from early high school, before ED took over. True happiness lies in the fact that I know I'm finally following my own insight. It lies in being in a relationship for the right reasons—not because I think having a man in my life will perfect it, but because he enhances it.

I won't ever depend on a man, or a clothes size, or anything external for my happiness again. For me happiness lies in the fact that now I know how to—and am willing to—feel pain, sadness, disappointment, anger, fear, joy, elation. I finally have my life back.

Julie: Declaring Independence

By the time she was forty, Julie had been "married" to ED for twenty-seven years. She'd been hospitalized twice, seen many different therapists, and had what she described as "a twelve-year incarceration in Overeaters Anonymous." ED was always able to woo her back—until she "filed for divorce."

I KICKED ED OUT—sure he phoned me, made threats on my life and sanity. He even showed up to threaten me at work. With the support of my therapist I continued to hang up on him and call my security officers (friends and family). After a while I decided to just get him off the street, so I tied him up and put him in the trunk of my car with a pair of cement galoshes on his feet. The plan: to dump him in the Pacific Ocean.

He rattled around in my trunk for a few months and I just turned up "Julie's" talk of how I fit into this world and how to take responsibility for my own actions and thoughts. I practiced all the skills I'd learned in my head and heart over the years.

Then my therapist let me know that I no longer had to define my life in ED terms—not "prerecovery," "recovery," "postrecovery," none of it. All that did was keep ED in my life.

So I filed for divorce. I took everything I wanted and dumped the rest into the ocean with ED and his cement galoshes.

It does not feel ecstatic to have killed ED, in fact it doesn't really feel like anything at all except what I know in my heart—what God knew all along: I've always been Julie, I'm Julie right now, and will be Julie forever. I am a fully whole person—recovered.

Are the Twelve Steps for You?
Pros and Cons of AA-based Programs for Eating Disorders

By Kristin von Ranson

Because eating disorders are often likened to addictions, many believe that the same methods used to treat addiction must be beneficial for people in recovery from eating disorders. In particular, the Twelve Step approach is considered by many to be a useful supplement to more targeted eating-disorder therapy.

Twelve Step programs, such as Overeaters Anonymous (OA) and Eating Disorders Anonymous, are self-help groups that follow the principles of Alcoholic Anonymous (AA). In OA, the words *food* and *compulsive eater* replace AA's words *alcohol* and *alcoholic*. Like individuals with alcoholism, those with food addictions are promised physical, emotional, and spiritual recovery if they follow the program's steps, tools, and traditions, which they learn by attending meetings. These steps call for members to recognize that they cannot control their addiction; to rely on a higher power; and to make amends for past behavior. Twelve Step groups are not led by professionals. Instead, members learn from more experienced members as part of a supportive fellowship of strugglers at various stages of recovery. Twelve Step meetings are low-cost and therefore are accessible even when other treatments aren't an option. Also, the Twelve

Step approach provides a focus on spirituality not found in most treatment programs.

Twelve Step programs are widely available; OA, for example, hosts as many as 6,500 meetings in seventy-five countries. But although the groups for eating disorders have many devotees, this philosophy is not for everyone. Some opponents recoil from what they feel is a cultlike fanaticism of Twelve Steppers, and agnostics and atheists may shy away from the approach's religious overtones. Critics argue that the similarities between eating disorders and chemical addictions are largely superficial and question the transfer of addiction treatments to eating disorders.

The most significant argument against applying the AA approach to eating disorders is the simple fact that abstaining from food is not a solution and, in fact, may be the very problem that needs to be overcome. While it's possible to live a healthy, happy life without ever drinking a drop of alcohol or using drugs, it's not possible to live without eating. For those whose illness is rooted in the idea of abstinence as a good thing, thinking about ED as an addiction might actually interfere with recovery.

Another concern is the lack of scientific evidence showing the impact of OA and similar programs. Little systematic research has been conducted on Twelve Step groups overall because of their emphasis on anonymity, and no studies have assessed how people with eating disorders, specifically, respond to the Twelve Step approach. While these groups can provide support and help some, they're certainly not for everyone in recovery, nor are they a substitute for professional therapy.

FIVE

Discovery

I F THE *RESTORATION* PHASE of recovery is equivalent to adolescence, then the phase that follows successful separation from ED can be likened to young adulthood. Now is the time for *discovery* of a uniquely fulfilling and meaningful life beyond ED. In this new life, perfection isn't defined by idealized weights, sizes, or grades but by individual passions and a sense of purpose. In this new life, you choose your own direction as a healthy, mature individual.

No timeline or medical chart can determine when you reach this stage. Some arrive within the first year after treatment, while others recover much more gradually. But sooner or later you'll begin to notice new adventures, insights, relationships, and pursuits emerging in ED's absence. Pay attention and enjoy them! These are the ultimate rewards of recovery.

Letters from readers in this discovery phase resound with love, curiosity, engagement, compassion, and also profound resilience. Most compellingly, they're enormously diverse, reporting on everything from art to rock climbing, dogs to dreams. Reading through them, I'm struck over and over again by the contrast between this mature diversity and the uniformity of letters I receive from individuals still in the throes of their eating disorders. It often seems as if everyone who falls prey to ED writes in the same lonely voice, but that as recovery progresses, the voices become ever more varied and richly individual. These letters tell me that the ability to raise one's true voice is a telling signal of recovery.

The perspective that accompanies this raised voice makes people in this stage of recovery a valuable force for societal and cultural change. Many become activists in the fights against eating and body-image disorders, sexual exploitation, consumerism, gender inequality, and weight and looks discrimination. Recovery can spark a broad range of activism because ED ties into so many different aspects of society. Not only do eating disorders represent a tragic waste of human potential, but as mental illnesses they're widely misunderstood. Meanwhile, the beauty, fashion, food, fitness, and advertising industries continue to perpetuate standards of perfection and consumption that directly contribute to the problem. Who better to fight for change than those who have personally suffered and triumphed over these devastating conditions?

When you've recovered, you know truths that others don't. You know that eating disorders are pervasive in every community, among men as well as among women, Hispanics and African-Americans as well as whites, lower-income as well as upper-income families, and throughout the world. You understand why they're universal—because of the primal nature of eating. Your experience has taught you that to eat is to live, and that to deny or distort the practice of eating signals pain so deep that it threatens survival. Regardless of what others may say, you know there's nothing voluntary or "chosen" about this pain, much less the desperate need to express it. And when you wake up to your own pain and develop the courage to work with it honestly and openly, you become an inspiration for others to transform their suffering into understanding. This is empowering, both for you and for those around you.

Your voice is also needed in order to overcome the stigma that surrounds and pigeonholes eating disorders as a problem limited to rich white girls and women, who supposedly have the luxury of "choosing" whether to eat too much or too little, or to "waste" food by purging. The power of your voice is strengthened by your past experience, because you understand, as others can't, that trivializing eating disorders is tantamount to trivializing suicide. You may also find it a tremendously empowering *new* experience to join a community fighting for such a personal cause.

At the same time, it's important to recognize that the stigma surrounding ED is a pervasive and persistent foe. Whether through doctors who belittle the problem of binge eating, designers who deny that their fashions promote anorexia, philanthropists who consider eating disorders unworthy of research funding, or insurance carriers who decline to cover adequate treatment for these illnesses, our society subtly demeans not only people with eating disorders but also those who fight against them.

The problem is not altogether external. I've been speaking out on this issue for decades, yet I constantly have to speak *over* echoes of this stigma within myself. My recovery from an eating disorder did not erase my judgmental nature. And stigma is a creature of judgment just as eating disorders are. I've found to my dismay that you can easily recover, only to aid and abet ED by belittling the relative importance of these illnesses, given the larger, graver, "more important" problems in the world. Why, you might ask yourself, should you spend energy fighting eating disorders when there are so many wars, polluted oceans, starving children, prisoners of conscience, brutal murders, pedophiles, hunted whales, endangered tribes, and other grave injustices? This question is the spawn of judgmental thinking, and I try to be mindful of the damage such thinking can do.

One of the benefits of recovery is that it frees us to pursue genuinely rewarding interests, to explore and address a broad range of challenges. You may well find that you'd rather *not* remain linked to ED as an activist. If so, I heartily encourage you to support whatever causes resonate most deeply for you. But there's a big difference between choosing alternative passions and missions, and treating the fight against eating disorders as an insignificant or minor cause. You don't have to be an activist to help change public perceptions about ED. All you have to do is speak the truth of your experience freely, frankly, and compassionately.

If we have the opportunity to help one person, save one life, or open one mind to the truth of these illnesses, there's no shame in seizing that opportunity and making a difference. As one letter reminded me, "There is no hierarchy to suffering." While none of us has the power to solve all the world's problems, each of us does have the power to change the world one person at a time—even if the only person we succeed in changing is ourself. It's *all* important work.

Pam: Compassion through Maturity

Pam, who struggled with eating disorders and substance abuse after losing her adoptive father at an early age and growing up with an anorexic mother, was only twenty-two when she wrote about her journey back to health in chapters 2 and 3. The most astonishing passages in her letters show a capacity for forgiveness that is rare, even among those who've never had an eating disorder. Her insights reveal just how closely compassion and maturity are intertwined—and how recovery can nurture both.

I WAITED A FEW YEARS after I was released from treatment to really make amends with my mother. Working on my relationship with her had to come after I worked on myself. I needed to be able to stand up for myself and let her know I was an adult.

Even if you aren't an adult yet, you need to make sure your parents understand you are your own person. As hard as that is for them to understand, they'll come around. It's only difficult because so many parents live through their child, as mine did.

My parents fought all the time. My father was a hardworking man. He was my hero. But my father cheated, and my mother cheated right back. She was so preoccupied with her weight, her looks, and her partying that she just didn't have time for a kid, but she always wanted one because she herself was adopted. After she had a partial hysterectomy, which left her unable to have her own, she adopted me.

She wasn't prepared for a real daughter. "I should never have adopted you, you were a terrible mistake" was repeated throughout my childhood. She wanted the *idea* of a child . . . basically, she wanted a doll.

It was complicated. I loved her, but part of me hated her for the love I felt for her. I had to do a lot of soul-searching to realize my mother had done the best she could. When I realized how her disorder had taken over her life, I told her, "Mom, you're severely anorexic. You don't see it, but you're just as sick as I am. Please get help, if not for you, for me."

She said, "Oh, I've been like this since I was a young girl. This is who I am. Can't you see that?"

I've had to learn that my mother will never be there when I need her, and if she says she'll be there, I know not to expect her. But once I understood my mother as a person, apart from the role of mother, it helped me realize she needs the same things I do.

It's so sad, but I do what any parent would with their child. I don't enable her by doing things for her anymore. I make her do things on her own, but when I know she can't and needs my help, I'm there for her. I let my hatred go, and I love her. I just make sure to teach her what I'm doing so she can do it for herself next time.

My mother and I have actually graduated from extremely superficial conversations to more emotionally in-depth ones. That only came from me setting boundaries with her. When I need her to be a mother, I tell her, "Mom, I need you to just listen. I need you to just tell me it will all be OK. You need to just say, 'I love you.' If you can't do that, I can call someone else, but I'd like it to be you."

I recently purchased a beautiful home with my boyfriend. She was irate. I stopped her. I said, "Mom, *you* settled down before *you* were ready. *You* wanted to party and have fun, to play and be free. *You* were not ready to settle down. I *am* ready. I want this house and all that comes with it. I want roots. They're what I've always wanted. I love you and I know you want the best for me, but what you're saying is what you want for *you*, not me. I'm not you, Mom. I'm me. You have to understand we're two separate people. If you can't be happy for me, you may call me back when you are . . . because you're not taking my happy feeling from me. It's mine."

She called me a week later and said she was happy for me.

I may get her as an adult, as a mother, for a few minutes or even an hour. I take all I can get. She's fragile, but she is trying and learning, just like I learned when I was in treatment. I love my mother. I no longer hate her or harbor anger toward her. She's who she is, and I am who I am.

Embracing the Mess
Opening up Your Definition of Recovery
By Bob Palmer

Once, the former British prime minister Harold Macmillan was asked what might threaten his plans for the future. He replied, "Events, dear boy, events." Even the prime minister's best-laid plans were vulnerable, because life itself is unpredictable. You might even call it messy.

When you have an eating disorder, you're always struggling against the messiness of life. But since everyone experiences messiness, it's not the mess or potential mess that distinguishes your illness. What's unique to the eating-disorder thought process is the belief that you could *avoid* the mess of life if only you could win the battle to control your body's weight and drive to eat.

Recovery from an eating disorder *is* possible. Certainly, most people recover in the sense that their weight returns to normal; they no longer binge, restrict, or purge; and their attitudes and beliefs become similar to those of people who've never had an eating disorder. Even individuals who've been quite ill generally recover to this degree. So, too, do people whose experience of ED is brief and who never seek professional help.

But is this true recovery? If you've recovered from an eating disorder, are you more likely than the next person to struggle with an eating disorder in the future? Yes. Is this inevitable? Certainly not. So how can you know when you're fully and truly recovered?

Some people cherish the conviction that they've put their eating disorder behind them forever and that it will never recur. They may feel they no longer have the ability or the motivation to fight with their body. This feeling is a good sign, and many prove to be correct in their conviction. But the best of all indicators of recovery may just be the acceptance that no one can know with absolute certainty what the future will bring.

The ability to embrace this universal uncertainty, yet get on with life nonetheless, is incompatible with the typical ED mind-set. Relapses may occur; they may not. You may see your plans through to completion; or you may replace them with others yet unforeseen. Remember Macmillan's "events" and their inherent unpredictability. Recovery means learning to enjoy the surprising mess of life.

Rhonda: Great Obsessions

Rhonda, a fifty-year-old social worker, began her recovery five years ago, after more than three decades of bulimia. Her ticket to health is the realization that she need not change her innate "obsessionality"; she just has to focus on channeling her energy toward positive, fulfilling, and purposeful obsessions!

I USED TO TELL my psychiatrist that I lacked the capacity for joy and that I simply sought the absence of pain. I've found surprisingly that my life is *filled* with joy and contentment! I still have thoughts that I'm unworthy at times, but I know where these thoughts come from, and they no longer have the power they once did. Yes, I'm still obsessional, but my new obsessions are purposeful and important, such as political change and social justice.

My experience tells me that bulimia is a dance of intimacy, pulling close and then pushing away. It's not about anger—as I was told constantly when I was suffering; it's about the intense need to be loved and cared for, and the terror that such closeness will engulf you and cause you to cease to exist as an individual person. I rebuilt myself from the outside in. At first it felt like a false self, but over time it's become me. I feel that the person I am to others is fairly in line with the person I know myself to be. I've been with my spouse eleven years, and we adopted a child from China seven years ago. Life is good and will only get better.

Erin: The Beauty of Imperfection

Erin, a photographer in her twenties, had wrestled with anorexia for fifteen years when intensive group therapy and weekly art therapy sessions helped her redefine what it meant to be an artist. For years she'd sought the "perfect" picture. Now she discovered the unexpected and often overlooked beauty around her. Drawing inspiration from Zen Buddhism and Eastern philosophy, she developed what she calls the aesthetic of imperfection.

In a little less than a year, Erin transformed her life. She started her own business, Erin Kroll Photography, a wedding and photojournalism and lifestyle photography company, and continues to work on an interactive photography exhibition, entitled Hope/Full: The Warrior Portraits, *celebrating the fullness of life in people who'd recovered from eating disorders. She launched Pink Dragonfly Clothing, an inspirational T-shirt company that supports eating disorder awareness and education. Also, seeing a need for eating disorders outreach in her community, she established a non-profit called Picture Imperfect, which helps young women develop an authentic voice and deeper sense of self through photography. Now thriving at thirty, Erin is living proof that creativity is too powerful an instrument to waste.*

MY EATING DISORDER pulled me away from myself and all the things that gave joy and meaning to my life. Unfortunately, photography was one of them. Chasing the impossible dream of "perfect," I was unable to grow as an artist. I was always trying to create the perfect piece, take the perfect shot, and wait for the perfect light, use the best equipment. It just wasn't happening. I continued to feel like a failure. Until I learned to let go with grace and dignity and accept imperfection, I simply couldn't appreciate the authentic beauty within and around me.

Picking up my camera again, returning to my creative roots, I felt like I was seeing everything for the first time. I felt more connected with the world around me, more patient and open. I felt alive. Each click of the shutter has freed me from the silence.

Somehow, it's become socially acceptable and expected of artists, especially photographers, to document tragedy, suffering, and the grotesque as a means to validate authenticity in the image and human experience. I'm not discounting the value that painful imagery have in our media, and I'm not denying the existence of suffering. I just want people to understand that there's another side to it all, another story to tell. I find the more I appreciate myself, the more I'm able to draw substance and soul into my images.

Katie: Discovering a Creative Career

Katie, now a freelance illustrator based in Bristol, UK, was treated for anorexia at age eighteen and thought herself recovered. But then she developed Binge Eating Disorder after being sexually abused. Full recovery from her eating disorders took another five years. Today, at twenty-six, Katie's still in therapy to resolve some aftereffects of the abuse. But Katie's therapy is also helping her creatively as she writes and designs a graphic novel based on her recovery. This project marks the launch of a new career that's as unexpected as it is rewarding.

IF YOU'D ASKED ME when I was seven years old what I wanted to do with my life, I wouldn't have hesitated to tell you that I wanted to write and illustrate books.

If you'd asked me when I was seventeen, I'd have said that I used to dream about being an illustrator but would never be good enough. By that time, I was entrenched in anorexia and had lost all belief in myself and my worthiness or ability to do what I dreamed of doing. By the time I graduated from university with a degree in Biology, I was struggling with binge eating and posttraumatic stress.

Looking back, it seems that I needed to reach that low point in order to make some serious decisions about my life. Deciding to pursue illustration was a major step in my recovery, but one that took me years to pluck up the courage for. For several months I felt suicidal, especially at the thought of entering the "real world" as an adult, having to work, having to grow up. I felt I had nothing to lose by making one last-ditch attempt to do what I wanted to do with my life. If it didn't work out, I told myself, I could give up then.

It felt like a step backward to start again at art college. Actually, it was one of the best decisions I've ever made. Having something to focus on that I was really passionate about helped my mood and my commitment to get better. Having come from a place where I had no self-esteem at all, it felt like a gift to be able to acknowledge my talents and put them to good use. Now illustration is my lifeblood, and I feel so lucky to have a job that pays me to do what I love. I still take myself by surprise sometimes with my willingness to show pride in what I do.

Working on my graphic novel is an experience of immense catharsis and relief, but I hope that the outcome reflects much more than that and becomes as useful to others as the writing process has been for me. I'd known right from the day I was diagnosed that I would write a book about my recovery. I came across too many books that told me I'd never fully recover from my illness, that it would always be lingering at the back of my mind. I made it my mission to find a way out. I had to believe that I could be completely well, or I would have given up on recovery altogether. I'm happy to say that it is indeed possible.

While I was unwell, I kept reams and reams of journals and imagined them becoming the book I wanted to write. Fortunately, I decided to burn them and lay aside the idea for a good while! It wasn't until I went to art college that I discovered how to tell my story.

The idea crystallized the day I read my very first graphic novel (Art Spiegelman's *Maus*). As I read, it was as if everything in my mind fell into place. I'm a visual thinker, so the idea of telling a story in pictures makes more sense, both in terms of how I process my thoughts and how I express myself. I also think it brings a different experience to the reader: more immediate, and yet more open to individual interpretation.

This project has been in my head for over nine years, and it feels like such a gift to be given the opportunity to write and publish it. It's a milestone that represents moving on from that stage of my life and starting my career as an artist. Although it will always be close to my heart because it's such a personal work, I hope it will be the first of many publications with my name on them.

My other work is not quite what I'd imagined as a little girl. Yes, I do paint and draw and make books, but I also maintain Web sites, organize exhibitions, budget and keep my own accounts, and relentlessly promote myself. I have to be prepared to work twelve-hour days or even longer, cope with difficult clients, and hardest of all, remain confident in my work in the face of rejection. I'm not sure if I've been able to do this because I've grown in confidence, or if doing all this is what's enabled me to grow.

I still feel like I'm growing, learning, reaching for my full potential both as an artist and as a person. But in other ways I've hardly changed at all. I'm still a highly obsessive person and a ruthless perfectionist. Working as an artist has taught me the benefits of these traits, in terms of my ability to organize my life, to evaluate my art, and to maintain the discipline it requires to work from home. I've had to learn to use these traits to my advantage without letting them consume or control me, to turn my weaknesses into strengths and assets.

Brenda: Venus Power!

Brenda struggled with disordered eating, chronic dieting, and a high weight throughout her first thirty-odd years. Along the way hundreds of diet books found their way to her bookshelves. Each diet stopped working as soon as she tired of the gimmick or novel way of

eating. Then Brenda would go back to her old ways and gain back
any weight she'd lost, and then some. Eventually she realized that
the diets themselves were actually making her fat. As an artist, she
decided to turn this discovery into the inspiration for a large and
powerful feminist art project.

MY PERSONAL EXPERIENCE inspired the Venus of Willendorf Project, an
ever-evolving series of feminist-activist art installations. The centerpiece
is a seven-foot-tall, five-foot-round papier-mâché statue, made entirely
from the pages of diet books, representing the prehistoric icon known as
the Venus of Willendorf, which until recently was believed to be the oldest
naturalistic representation of a human being. A landscape created from
the high-gloss pages of cookbooks surrounds her. Smaller figures of the
Venus in the installation are each made from copies of books by a single
best-selling diet-book author; for example, there's an Atkins Diet Venus
and a Dr. Phil Diet Venus.

In the 1960s the Venus of Willendorf was adopted by the feminist art
movement as a symbol of female power, for her presence was physical
evidence of a time when women were revered as divinities. Her large,
voluptuous form added credence to feminists' arguments against insti-
tutionalized beauty standards. She has been and continues to be used to
promote size acceptance, fertility, and the earth mother. But sadly, as I did
research on the Venus of Willendorf, I found that her image has become a
vehicle for selling the ideas of an increasingly fat-phobic society. In fact, the
most potent catalyst for my project was a very short-lived TV commercial
for a diet system: a man's voice-over droned on about the dangers of obesity
while a picture of the Venus of Willendorf rotated on the screen. The voice
asked viewers if they really wanted to look like her. The diet industry had co-
opted one of the most powerful symbols in women's history as a means of
selling self-hatred and promoting patriarchal body-loathing ideals.

Regardless of how modern society views the Venus of Willendorf,
she's by far the most realistic representation of my physical body that I've
seen in the public domain—far more realistic than the images one sees in
fashion magazines or in film and television. I decided to make her the centerpiece of my art, thereby reclaiming her as an honest depiction of what
dieting and weight obsession do to the human body.

Papier-mâché as a medium has special significance for this piece.

Papier-mâché is a French term that means "chewed paper," an ideal metaphor to describe how I devoured diet books in my earlier years. Making them into papier-mâché seemed a fitting end for these books. I wanted them destroyed and virtually unreadable except for some of the type on the outer layers of the finished piece—evidence of their original purpose.

Discarded diet books are the sole source for the papier-mâché from which my project is constructed. I go to garage and yard sales and scour used bookstores and recycle centers, but the Internet has proved to be the best source. Not only have I been able to find large numbers of books online, but the Web has helped me spread the word about my project worldwide (www.fatfeministactivistartist.wordpress.com). People as far away as India have contributed to the piece, taking part in the installation's creation.

Once I was ready to start building my central Venus, I hosted "The Great Diet Rip-up" at my studio. The event brought our local community together in a hands-on experience of diet-book ripping and page pasting, both a performance and an interactive art project to create the voluptuous curves of the large figure. One benefit of working with papier-mâché is that it's lightweight. But with each subsequent layer it becomes stronger and increases in weight. This works as a physical metaphor for what happened to me with each subsequent diet: I gained more and more weight with each diet I tried. With each diet book added, the Venus, too, gains weight.

The central Venus figure is compiled from different books, including at least one copy of each book used to make smaller Venus pieces. There's a separate inventory for this central piece, as well as an inventory for each of the smaller ones. A bibliography catalogs the books used in the project as a whole.

One often reads about the multibillion-dollar diet industry, but what does that mean? To see it in paper, to experience a room filled with pages and pages of books, might really change how one thinks about dieting in the future. When people visually experience the volume of the issue by standing at the center of this installation, they can feel the weight and the pressure in both a physical and an intellectual way.

I have no intention of neutralizing the subject; I want to be identified as revealing my femaleness and my fatness. My hope is that my project will lead to the knowledge that diets don't work and that it's no longer necessary for women to maintain an androgynously slender figure in order to qualify as beautiful, worthwhile, valuable human beings. I now have the freedom to make art like a woman and I now have the freedom to have hips and a belly and breasts like a woman. I am the Venus!

Moving Beyond Weight
Staying Healthy at Every Size
By Deb Burgard

Dieting doesn't result in lasting weight loss for most people. Instead, many develop a cycle of losing and regaining that actually keeps ratcheting their weight higher, leaving them less healthy in the end. Dieting teaches us to ignore the most reliable coach we have in making decisions about food: our own bodies. And without our body coach we become vulnerable to food marketing, physical shame and dissatisfaction, and disordered eating.

Having found our culture's persistent focus on weight loss to be frustrating and counterproductive, health care professionals and patients developed the "Health at Every Size" model to encourage good health at whatever weight is normal and natural for your individual body. The general components of HAES include the following:

- Access to highly valued food, eaten in harmony with hunger and fullness
- Access to regular and pleasurable physical activity
- Access to restful sleep
- Access to quality time with loved ones
- Activisim to rid the cultural environment of weight stigma, discrimination, violence, and the assignment of moral worth to health (healthism)

By exchanging the goal of weight loss for the goal of health and positive quality of life, the HAES approach can help you transcend the restricting-versus-bingeing, good-versus-bad polarities. HAES instead offers the possibility of a peaceful and even loyal relationship with your body, not as the target of blame and shame but rather as an essential partner in health and well-being.

Health at Every Size resources include the following:

ORGANIZATIONS

Association for Size Diversity and Health (ASDAH), www.sizediversityandhealth.org

Society for Nutrition Education, Weight Realities Division, www.sne.org

LinkedIn Intuitive Eating Professionals, www.linkedin.com/groups?gid=1806863

WEB SITES AND BLOGS

www.HAEScommunity.org

www.BodyPositive.com

BOOKS

Bacon, Linda. *Health at Every Size: The Surprising Truth about Your Weight.* Dallas: BenBella Books, 2009.

Matz, Judith, and Ellen Frankel. *The Diet Survivor's Handbook.* Naperville, Ill.: Sourcebooks, 2006.

Kylie: ED or Improv?

Kylie underwent three months of treatment for anorexia and bulimia in 2008. She didn't expect to find that experience very funny, but to her surprise, she found it therapeutic to laugh at it. Since then, she's discovered that humor is actually her personal key to true health.

ALTHOUGH ONE SHOULD NEVER doubt the gravity and life-threatening aspects of eating disorders, when I was in treatment, I'd make fun of myself in order to bring lightness to my situation. On top of the expressive sessions of art therapy, I wrote down funny quotes, composed mocking poems and songs, decorated and named my feeding tube. I watched one of my fellow patients throw cans of Ensure at the trees. We painted T-shirts advertising the treatment program with sayings like, "I came for the food."

Upon leaving, I vowed to keep up not only the arts and crafts but also my sense of humor. I took advantage of my background in acting and signed up for improv-theater classes. Improv requires one to live in the moment, and to make up scenes and characters on the spot. This has proven to be one of my greatest motivators for recovery.

When I was consumed (pardon the pun) with my eating disorder, I always worried about what I'd eaten in the past, or what I'd eat in the future; how much I weighed yesterday, and how much I'd weigh tomorrow at the nutritionist's office. I could never get out of my head and just be. Improv has helped me get outside the obsessions. I become a character and instantaneously lose the eating-disorder identity. I live moment-to-moment, and not in the past or future.

Another healing aspect of improv is the hilarity. Laughing and making others laugh is the biggest natural high for me—bigger than the high I once had from restricting, bingeing and purging, and losing weight. It brings real joy to me and to others.

Improv and eating disorders can never coexist. You need energy to perform improvised scenes. Lots of it. One day I didn't eat enough before my class, and I didn't have the energy to throw myself entirely into my characters and scenes. I realized I had to make a choice: the eating disorder or improv?

Ultimatums are extremely powerful. I always believed I could have it all—a thin body as well as my creativity. However, after that one lousy class, I realized I couldn't have it all. My quick wit and active brain are shot without food. I had to make the choice. After a period of trial and error, I chose recovery.

In order to perform, on stage and in life, I have to eat and maintain a certain weight. In order to laugh, I need to stay healthy. There's absolutely nothing comedic about an emaciated body. Improv embraces life and all its insanity. And so will I.

Amy: The Power of Mentorship

Amy struggled with eating disorders throughout her teens and early twenties. Now twenty-six, she's living a life she never could have imagined when she completed treatment three years ago. The key to her new life is relationship, but that word means something entirely different to her now than it used to.

I WENT TWO YEARS without being in a relationship with a guy. I spent those two years getting to know who I was and what I really liked doing. I found that I liked painting, pottery, hiking, and being a role model.

I started a weekly eating-disorders support group and eventually I had women who were struggling looking up to me and calling me for support from a variety of locations, including a state prison for women.

I moved twelve hundred miles from home to work at a treatment center. I run a weekly body-image group and have made great new friends in my short time in this new location. I wouldn't have been able to make this move alone if I was still stuck in my eating disorder.

My advice to anyone attempting to recover is don't quit before the miracle happens. It usually gets worse before it gets better, but it does get better. If you have been in recovery for a while and find yourself struggling, tell someone! Do not be ashamed. Stay connected with others in recovery.

READY, GET SET, SUPPORT!
Advice for Setting Up Your Own Support Group
By Susan Ringwood

Support groups facilitated by volunteers who've been through similar life events can provide a safe place to share experiences, worries, and coping skills. By setting up a support group, you can enrich your own life as well as making a positive difference on others'.

Here are some simple pointers to help establish your group, and some potential risks to consider:

- The urge to help others is strong, and some people try to take this on when their own lives are still so affected by the eating disorder that their energies can get dangerously drained. Better to wait until you have the strength to give to others, rather than risk your own health.
- Having at least two volunteer leaders working together will reduce the demands on your time and energy and make you more effective in the support you give to others.
- Be realistic about how often you can meet. One to two hours early on a weekday evening seems to suit most people best. Having a regular time and place you can publicize will help to get the group established.
- Choose a neutral public space to meet, such as a library meeting room, a church basement, or some other community facility. Some groups may run as adjuncts to a particular treatment facility.
- Think carefully before making your personal-contact details freely available. You may prefer to create an e-mail account specifically to handle group communication.
- Will you charge for attending, or ask for voluntary donations toward the costs of room rental, refreshments, and so on? Most people prefer to pay their own way, and you can always use discretion to ensure that no one's excluded for financial reasons.
- It can be challenging to have families and sufferers in the group at the same time. Some groups offer alternate meetings—families one week, sufferers the next. Some organize around the types of condition; others include anyone no matter their diagnosis. Find out what's most comfortable for your group.
- You may find there are legal constraints on providing support to young people without their parents present. In the UK, for example, volunteers working with those under sixteen must get certificates showing that criminal-background checks have been done.
- Will you have speakers and set topics, or will people attend for personal support only? Will you campaign and lobby for better services? Groups that have a mix of some structured time with less formal networking support seem to suit most people well.

- Are treatment professionals invited or excluded? Some groups have found it helpful to invite speakers from the treatment professions at times, or to bring a professional advisor to the group.
- Is there a mental-health organization in your community that you could affiliate with? They may have meeting rooms, training, or other support to offer. Make contact with other local groups, even if they're supporting a different issue, as they may still have help to offer.
- Have simple ground rules that anyone attending the group agrees to adhere to. This will help you conduct an effective and safe meeting. This is particularly the case if a group member tends to dominate the time, or is otherwise difficult to accommodate. Be fair, be firm, and be decisive. If you have to say no, mean it.
- Use the local press and media to publicize your group. Release good-news stories about how families have beaten an eating disorder, along with your group's meeting time and place. It gives hope and encouragement to others facing similar challenges.

The Resources section at the end of the book includes links to Web sites where you can get more information on running a support or self-help group.

Merry: Simple Play

Merry is the fifty-one-year-old wife, nurse, and mother who described her experience with dialectical-behavior therapy in chapter 3. Now, restored to health, she's continually amazed by the rediscovery of dreaming, daydreaming, and simple play.

I HAVE SO MANY THINGS I want to do in life now. I'd love to have enough money to go back to college and major in English and Art. I want to learn French. I want to play more. I want to give myself permission to slow down, to quiet the overambitious part of me.

I'm so in love with my husband! I'd love to travel around the world with him. I want to make cookies with future grandchildren. I want to play with Play-Doh with them, even if it makes a mess on the floor. Making sand castles at the beach with them, lying on our backs in the backyard on the grass looking at clouds will be fun. I want to teach them that they're important and that mistakes are an opportunity to learn something new.

We have the power to make a difference. I hope to increase public awareness of eating disorders through my art—making quilts using thread-painting. (Thread-painting means painting a picture using a sewing machine, just like a child paints in a coloring book.) It's what I do for play, without an inner critic.

I am also writing a book for teens with eating disorders, focusing on self-acceptance and recovery using DBT skills. I want to show them that trust and hope are not just empty words in a dictionary.

Whitney: The Exuberant Extrovert

Whitney had been out of treatment a little over a year when she paused to reflect on the changes in her life and in her sense of self. Exuberance is my word, not hers, but it's difficult to imagine a better one to describe her irrepressible spirit.

IF I HADN'T had the experiences that came as a result of my eating disorder, I wouldn't be as strong as I am now. I probably wouldn't appreciate life as much as I do now. I'm learning to love the person I'm becoming.

Before starting recovery, I was afraid to go anywhere with people, especially anywhere there'd be food. I was self-conscious and didn't want anyone to know how lonely I was—I couldn't show my weakness. Yet since starting on my road to recovery, I've discovered that I'm a people person! Who knew?

Everyone has an interesting story, and if you show an interest in what they have to say, they'll talk to you. Make a friend! And if someone doesn't want to talk or is rude for some reason or another, move on to someone else. That was hard for me at first. But you just have to forget about that one person so you can move on.

Also since beginning recovery, I found out I have a true passion for the outdoors. Rock climbing, rappelling, hiking, all of it. I was never supposed to enjoy that stuff. I thought I was supposed to be a dud. But that's not true. I'm supposed to enjoy living. I'm supposed to be passionate, friendly, extroverted, short, blue-eyed, brown-haired, smart—everything God blessed me with is who I'm supposed to be. If that means I get to enjoy rock climbing and getting dirty, that's me. If that means I like dressing up and going to the ballet with a friend for a girls' night, that's me.

Happiness can't be found in a mirror. Happiness is found in what you do, who you're with, and what you can do for other people. Instead of asking "why?" ask "why not?" If you can't think of a good reason why not, go for it. A friend once told me, "I don't understand you. You like the city and all that stuff, but you're outdoorsy, too. You're environmentally dyslexic." That was the best compliment someone could have given me! I have a vast array of interests. I'm wonderfully complex.

I've learned to be passionate about taking chances. Five months after I started climbing, instead of attending my own college graduation in December, eight (very responsible) friends and I rappelled the deepest free-fall pit in North America—Ellison's Cave near Lafayette, Georgia. At Christmas that year, I flew to Alaska to meet some friends and explore the final frontier! I flew a small plane. We went ice climbing on tremendous, beautiful glaciers! We skied out to an ice-covered lake in the wilderness and camped there—on top of the ice-covered lake! I learned to ski in the dark in the Alaskan wilderness. Alaska is truly breathtaking in the wintertime. And life is beautiful.

Looking back, I can't believe I let myself be alone for so long. I love people. And you know what? People genuinely like me. I had no idea!

Niki: Discovering Awareness through the Body

> *Niki is an artist who had her third flare-up of anorexia in her mid-thirties while trying to conceive a child. Finally, she succeeded in giving birth to a healthy baby. Determined to set a good example for her son, she committed herself to recovery. In the process she discovered that her body had a great deal to teach her, not only about herself but about her entire family.*

I'M A HAIR TWIRLER, and have been since even before my eating disorder. My dad was a compulsive runner for many years and ran himself into two foot surgeries. My mom just started an antidepressant for anxiety. My younger brother has gotten as big as a house by becoming a bodybuilder.

He gets totally freaked out when he weighs less than his ideal. His bodybuilding is all-consuming. When he's getting ready for a competition, he often can't hold down a job because of all the eating, lifting, and cardio. I'm certain he's sterile from the steroids, and he's even taken things like thyroid medications without having a thyroid condition. He was once in counseling, but when asked to give up compulsive lifting, he instead gave up counseling. It breaks my heart when I look at him.

For a long time I wondered how two kids could come from the same parents and be so different, but after all, we were just the same. Missing the same essential part, just expressing it through our bodies in different ways: anorexia as a profound way of not being there, and bodybuilding a profound and undeniable being there, just masking the same sense of self-doubt and lack of self-acceptance. I was trying to disappear, and he was trying to get so big that my dad would have to see him.

With bodybuilding I think it's a lot easier to negatively judge the money spent, the steroid use, the self-centeredness, because it seems to be all about vanity. When you look at an anorexic, the response is, "Oh, she's sick." But both conditions are about wanting to be perfect, and when you see the similarities, it's much easier to be compassionate. We have each spent most of our lives engaged in our behaviors, and both felt a real sense of loss when we acknowledged those behaviors no longer served us.

I've had a really interesting experience lately with my belief about my body. My husband and I moved our family to Minnesota this summer, and I really wanted to just go into my eating disorder in order to deal with the stress, but I couldn't. It was like the brain chemistry was different.

Then I found a practitioner of the Feldenkrais Method. That's one method of somatic education, also called Awareness Through Movement. It has been fascinating. I know that my eating disorder was about denying my body, but I didn't realize all the smaller ways I wasn't in my body. For instance, I'd hold my breath. When working with the Feldenkrais Method, I realized my subconscious thought was that unless I held my breath I might make a mistake, and then I wouldn't be perfect. I found I had absolutely no awareness of my pelvis or backside—that I was really one-sided and in my head.

The amazing thing about the process, or the lessons, is that the more you try, the less you learn. And the more you try, the quieter your body gets, and the louder your mind gets with all the self-talk you (well, I) almost never hear because it's so ingrained. I'm trying to find a way to live in my body with the feelings I'm so uncomfortable with, without finding other methods of self-abuse. I think my lesson has really been to accept my body as a vehicle for being me.

Inner Workings
Body-Awareness and Movement-Awareness Tips and Resources
By Beth Shelton

Sometimes when you have an active eating disorder, it's difficult to feel yourself inside your body. You may start to experience your body as an object that can only be viewed and judged from the outside. Recovery can reignite your ability to sense your body from the inside, through pleasurable sensations, feelings, and movement.

Simply moving, breathing, and attending to your body in stillness or in action can put you back in touch with the joy of living. Reconnecting with your body can help you handle emotions and give you new strength, vitality, and self-understanding. Also, people sometimes need to relearn a gentle, self-nurturing approach to movement, because this part of their life has been overtaken by ED's compulsive exercise.

A variety of body-mind practices offer safe ways for you to learn to

- Enjoy and appreciate your physical self
- Move more easily and with more pleasure
- Sense and accept your immediate feelings and emotions
- Feel more comfortable in your own skin

The Alexander Technique (www.alexandertech.org)

As a student of the Alexander Technique you'll work with a practitioner individually or in a group, focusing especially on the relationship between your head and spine. This method involves you in a gentle process of becoming more aware of your own movement patterns as you learn to release tension and move in an easier, more grounded way.

The Feldenkrais Method (www.feldenkrais.com)

Feldenkrais work will help you increase your body awareness and explore new types of movement. In group sessions, you'll learn movement sequences and focus deeply on sensations and connections inside your body. In individual sessions, the practitioner will work with you on your own particular movement patterns.

Dance/Movement Therapy (www.adta.org)

In Dance/Movement Therapy you'll learn to use movement as a form of psychotherapeutic healing. The therapist will guide you in exploration of your thoughts and feelings through movement, giving you an opportunity for reflection, self-expression, and deepened self-understanding.

Sara: New Dreams

Sara began her recovery from anorexia and bulimia during college. Eleven years later, she realized that her eating disorder had forced her to give up one set of expectations, but recovery had empowered her to pursue opportunities that were both more challenging and more rewarding than any of the "perfect" fantasies from her earlier life.

THE REAL SARA is emerging, much like a butterfly pushing out of the cocoon that caused its metamorphosis. I'm learning to be patient with myself, to care for and trust myself—not an easy task after so many years of betrayal. However, among all the struggles, triumphs, setbacks, and celebrations, there's one thing I know for sure: my heart will not lead me astray. This new direction will lead me to my true dreams. Not the white picket fence in my head, but the dreams sitting dormant in my heart, waiting for me to hear them.

After spending much of my life being the person I thought I should be, I discovered parts of myself that didn't follow what my head (that is, ED, society, family, religion, and so on) deemed permissible. In spite of all the great occupations I had the potential for, or that would earn far more money, I realized my passion is for working with children. I discovered how I could be spiritual without just following rules or succumbing to the consumer religion of many Americans. And finally, I'm starting to honor my own dreams for my future: writing a book, teaching children in Africa, inspiring others to overcome addictions, falling in love, climbing mountains, becoming a professor, connecting with others, and living mindfully.

As time passes, my dreams may change or be redefined, but I will always follow my heart. And when the distinction between my head and heart gets fuzzy, I turn to writing, nature, or art for clarification—all things that calm my spirit and quiet the noise.

My ten-year college reunion was this past summer; unfortunately, I wasn't able to attend. It occurred at the same time I was moving to Colorado. After living on the prairie of South Dakota for twenty-eight years, I felt I was being called by Colorado with its majestic mountains and endless sunshine! I didn't know a single person there, yet my heart knew it was time for a new adventure.

I don't have a minivan or white picket fence. I have a small apartment overlooking the mountains. I spend my days teaching five-year-olds, and my weekends climbing mountains with friends. Far from what I imagined ten years ago, this new life is picture-perfect in my heart!

Celia: A Passion for Activism

Celia entered treatment for anorexia shortly after beginning college. Her recovery has been life-changing in every respect. Less than two years later this once-introverted young woman embarked upon a crusade.

THERE'S A NEW DIMENSION to my battle: trying to open a dialogue about eating disorders. On a campus of forty-thousand-plus students, there are limited (and that's being generous) resources for people with eating disorders, even though ED is everywhere—at the gym, in my Women's Studies class, at every turn. When I tell people this, they assume I'm struggling and that seeing these girls makes it harder for me. Quite the contrary. I'm in no way triggered by these girls. I love my life, my body, my health, and I do not want to go back there. If there's one passion in my life, above all else, it is my recovery.

If I told you all the things people say to me when I ask them about campus resources or plans of action for dealing with eating disorders, you'd be outraged. Trainers at the gym, resident advisors, close friends, even counselors at the campus women's center (!!!)—the policy is, "It's not our job." *Infuriating!*

I'm going to speak to my four-hundred-person Women's Studies class, to offer hope to the countless people in that class alone who are struggling.

I am completely comfortable discussing my story, my fight, with anyone. I think that openness and honesty are the two most important elements of recovery. I'd like to think I'm breaking down the stigma, one conversation at a time.

Lead On!
Become an Activist
By Theresa Fassihi and Kitty Westin

Being well involves much more than eating normally and maintaining a healthy weight. Along with physical and emotional well-being, a sense of purpose, empowerment, and meaning plays a vital role in recovery. As you recover, you may discover a creative streak or talent you didn't even know you had. Perhaps you find your true passion working with animals or children, or spending time with loved ones who felt cut off from you in the depths of your illness. Your passion may also prompt you to become an advocate for those still struggling with ED.

Perhaps you feel that your hard-earned experience deserves to be put to some positive use. Maybe you want to motivate and inspire those in the early stages of recovery. Or, you'd like to become active in the fight for more funding and research, better treatment, and greater public awareness around eating disorders. This feeling of wanting to give back is a sign of health. Activate it!

Activism will help you add new dimension to your life and can give you a profound feeling of satisfaction. You'll build rewarding relationships with fellow advocates and the people you help. And you can be sure that your energy and experience are sorely needed.

Here are just a few of the many ways you can make a difference in the fight against eating disorders:

- Assist with or form a local self-help or support group.
- Start a recovery blog or join an existing online recovery support forum to share your experience and encourage others.
- Make your voice heard in the media by writing letters to the editor of your local newspaper or calling in to local call-in radio shows when the topic of eating disorders appears in the news.
- Join a politically active organization to work for change in the quality and accessibility of eating-disorder treatment and research
- Become an active member of the Academy for Eating Disorders (www.aedweb.org) or your regional or national eating-disorder education and awareness organization. (See the Resources section for a list of organizations.)
- Offer to partner with local treatment facilities to organize public-awareness activities in your region.
- Work with your school, university, or local hospital to develop education and awareness services for eating disorders.

SIX

Wise Minds

L OOKING BACK at one's now-distant eating disorder is like reflecting on a child. Full recovery turns ED into a slice of history and, perhaps, a window into your past, but it's no longer a malevolent force with the immediate power to destroy you. Those who wrote letters at this late stage often noted connections and solutions that had eluded them when they were ill. Many found particular solace in the fact that even personality traits that once fueled their illness, such as perfectionism and persistence, could be trained in health to serve truly fulfilling goals.

We now know that eating disorders are biologically based mental illnesses. We know that DNA determines who's likely to develop an eating disorder and who's not. And we know that eating disorders can be distress signals—symptoms—of much deeper and more complex syndromes of personality, stress, and behavior. Recovering from an eating disorder won't transplant our personality or rid our lives of anxiety. It won't cure all that ails us, and it certainly won't make us, or our lives, perfect and problem-free. But recovery will make us stronger, more resilient, and more resourceful as we face life's inevitable ups and downs.

No one knows the truth about recovery better than those who have themselves fully recovered. I've received letters from many of these "wise minds" who've chosen to stay active in the fight against eating disorders. They come from male as well as female therapists who find that their own experience of ED helps them help their patients; researchers whose personal experience motivates them to find scientific answers and solutions for eating disorders; and individuals who offer their own personal recoveries as inspiration for others.

In their varied ways, these letters prove that with time, patience, and compassion, full recovery is within reach for everyone. Ultimately, they also echo the wisdom of the artist Sister Corita Kent, whose advice was, "Love the moment. Flowers grow out of dark moments. Therefore, each moment is vital. It affects the whole. Life is a succession of such moments and to live each is to succeed."

Maya: Hope Born of Despair

When Maya's letter came to me from Israel, I was stunned by her story of recovery and resilience. I open this chapter with Maya because she demonstrates so powerfully the human capacity for hope, love, growth, and survival that ED tries so insistently to destroy. Her example also proves that these great strengths can triumph over almost any odds. Maya is now forty-three, happily married, and the mother of three. She is a psychotherapist who works with geriatric patients.

IT IS WITH GREAT PRIDE and hope that I am sharing the short version of my life story with you. Pride for having battled ED and overcoming it, and hope that my recovery may provide a ray of hope for those still in the midst of this ongoing struggle for health.

I was born on a kibbutz, the eldest of four children. Throughout my childhood and on to the first years of puberty I managed to be everything I was expected to be. A "good girl," I played the cello with promising talent, performed well in school, helped at home.

At the age of fourteen I was brutally raped. I felt alone in a shattered world, and couldn't find a single soul to share my horror and pain. I prayed that someone would notice my wounds and tend to me, but no matter how hard I tried, no one ever guessed. Bit by bit, all I'd held dear prior to the event began to crumble. I began having difficulties in school and couldn't find the concentration for my music. I began having sex with various men, seeking acknowledgment and revenge. My parents wanted to help, but couldn't figure it out, and mostly expressed disappointment at what had become of me. Our relationship was one of mutual disappoint-ment.

I turned to food. I ate to feel full, to distract my thoughts, and—now I know—to become someone undesirable enough to be safe from the male sex. After a period of eating, I was so fat that I couldn't bear to see myself.

In a search for self-control, I began to diet. I lost half my body weight within a very short period of time, and without even knowing, I became addicted to the feeling of needing no one, needing nothing. Death seemed a path to the end of pain and loneliness. When I became too weak to func-tion, I was hospitalized.

My parents stood by me, baffled by the turn my life had taken, but fighting for my life nonetheless. I looked in their eyes and saw pain. The "good girl" within me felt guilty and the dilemma arose: starve myself for me, or eat for them. I did both, traveling back and forth on the road between recovery and suicide.

After finishing my tour of duty in the Israeli army, I left the kibbutz to try my luck in the big city. With a dollar in my pocket and nowhere to sleep, I began working as a high-class escort girl, turning into the exact opposite of what I should have become. I led a double life, working as a waitress during the day, but earning my keep during the night. I managed to be what I was expected to be and at the same time to lead a full secret life with a language of its own.

One warm summer evening, I met Abir. Within a few hours, he moved in with me. Abir wanted to know me. He wanted to listen. He looked at me and I felt beautiful and unique. The night we met, I left the escort agency, never to return.

We got married a few weeks later. I told him the story of my life—the rape, the men, and the escort chapter. I left nothing untold. He held my hand, looked at me with all the love in the world, and said, "You must be the most courageous woman I've ever met, to have endured all that alone."

For the first time in my life, being loved, appreciated, and accepted for who I am, I could finally be myself and take pride in being me. Being loved and appreciated without being judged, releasing the false self that had become my permanent mask and replacing it with a truer version of myself—all that came with time. I felt as if something that had been cut off for years was coming back to life and renewing its growth process. This enormous love was my first and biggest step toward recovery.

Within the frame of a loving relationship, I felt some inner peace. The turbulence was at ease, the anger fading. I felt safe enough, fulfilled to a point I could take the next step.

The second step to recovery was facing my mother, whom I have loved and hated with all my might. I sat with her on the eve of my first child's birth. I looked at her with the love I now had within me and told her that I believe she loves me and never meant to hurt me. I asked her to forgive me for any pain I might have inflicted upon her and said I forgive her for all the pain she inflicted upon me. I did not need her to acknowledge my hurt or apologize for it. My forgiveness was a way of putting past anger behind me, leaving yet more room for love. My mother, the most incredible woman I know, embraced this gesture of mine, joining me on a journey to a healthy, loving, and mature mother-daughter relationship. I suppose it's true that the best way to change someone is by accepting them for who they are . . .

The third step was to find my way back to normalcy. Having led the life I did, this was not to be taken lightly. After giving birth to my third child, I was going through a crisis. Having gained a lot of weight during my pregnancy, searching for my purpose in life other than being a wife and a mom, I began therapy.

I was fortunate to find a therapist with a unique capacity to see the best in me and mirror it back to me within a secure and trusting relationship. She was a source of great power and growth. Within a short while, something shifted inside me. Abir sensed this change. He took me by the hand as I registered at the university.

Together, he and I managed to raise three young children while I held a steady job and successfully graduated with my BA. I was than accepted to an MA program, and continued to study another three years of psychodynamic psychotherapy. I had become a therapist, gaining appreciation from friends, family, and peers. At last, I was just like everybody else.

This joining with the "mainstream world" offered me a sense of belonging and allowed me to rebuild my self-worth. Little by little, my superiority over ED was being reinforced. I had too much to lose if I gave in to the temptation of my symptoms. The more you have, the harder you'll fight to maintain it.

I'm proud to say that after years of battling ED, I am fully recovered. To me, being recovered means looking in the mirror and seeing someone with a few more pounds to lose, regardless of how much I weigh. It means having some self-doubt and minor insecurity arising every now and again. It means having a special and complicated relationship with food, probably forever. But more than this, it means loving and accepting myself *with* all of that. It means knowing, deep inside, that no matter how hard it gets and how tempting it may be to go back to the old behaviors, I will never give in to them again. I will always remain in some form of struggle with my disorder, but I will triumph, always. I have full faith in that. I am me, I am loved for being me. Nothing is more powerful than that.

For those who still struggle, for those standing by them, there is hope. We have the opportunity to mold our life through the choices we make. I truly believe that love, acceptance, forgiveness, and a deep sense of purpose can help you overcome this struggle.

Kim: Make Your Own Miracle

Kim Lampson has been free of her eating disorder for twenty-five years and is now a psychologist in private practice in Washington State, but she still vividly recalls the process of recovery. Hers is a message of hope.

I'M AN INTELLIGENT PERSON, a great student, and a competent, creative woman of strong faith. Even so, my recovery is my greatest personal accomplishment. It took me ten years to change my distorted thinking, learn to eat without fear again, and regain the weight I'd lost in ten months. It was as though I'd had a massive stroke that left me unable to think normally about food or weight. I had to start over.

Now, thirty years after my darkest eating-disorder days, it's quiet inside. There's room for thinking new thoughts and room for feeling new feelings. Although I'm more aware of my shortcomings, my life is more consistent with my faith. Sure, my eating and weight are normal now, but it's the inner transformation that carries the most weight. It took a decade of hard work to change my mind.

Is it a day-to-day struggle? No. Will I ever go back? No. Why? I don't want to. The answer sounds so simple, but often the simplest of statements are the most profound. My mind is filled with other things now. Thoughts, passions, feelings, dreams, and ideals. I exercise to stay strong; I eat anything I want; my BMI is in the healthy range; I appreciate my body.

Long-term recovery is not a miracle bestowed on some and not on others. If you want it, you have to change your lifestyle to make it possible. Here are eight of the many factors that I believe help sustain recovery:

1. Choose to be responsible for someone or something other than yourself. Take care of a sick relative, raise a child, have pets.

2. Choose to love someone or something beyond your family of origin—a life partner, a friend, God. Then, be willing to feel. With relationships come feelings. To be recovered, you have to be willing to feel and no longer use behaviors to numb out.

3. Develop a meaningful passion that competes with the eating disorder and allows you to connect with people—music, acting, writing, gardening, to name a few.

4. Continually challenge yourself to grow until you value yourself. People take care of what's precious to them.

5. Find an activity that allows you to appreciate your healthy body's strength and power. Dance, ski, swim, lift weights (in moderation, of course!).

6. Work on recovery until you can eat anything you want. People tend to want what they can't have, so don't absolutely deny yourself anything.

7. Surround yourself with people healthier than you are. Don't deny yourself friends with eating disorders, but have more who've never struggled with food issues.

8. Develop your spirituality. Replace the scale-god. Find a belief system that gives your life purpose and meaning.

I don't believe that you and I were "given" an eating disorder so that we could help others, or to teach us some great cosmic lesson. I had an eating disorder because I blindly stumbled on an illusion of control, safety, and self-worth that insulated me from my feelings and met my needs at the time. However, I have chosen to use what I learned from this bizarre kind of suffering to become wiser, to help others, and to make the world a better place.

Angela: Alive and Engaged

Angela Schaffner struggled with anorexia and bulimia in college. Now thirty-three, she's a psychologist at the Atlanta Center for Eating Disorders, an outpatient treatment center for eating disorders in Atlanta, Georgia. For Angela, recovery is an ongoing act of faith.

ONE OF THE GREATEST parts of recovery is that I can now pour my energy into worthwhile pursuits such as loving and raising my son, enjoying my relationship with my husband, providing therapy, offering hope to clients, growing in relationships with extended family and friends, and allowing myself to be more fully known by other people. For years I felt so passive and fearful, never good enough. Now I'm still fearful sometimes, but I seek to connect with other people rather than distancing and isolating myself from them. I see the ways that I shine and have begun to treat myself more like I treat my son, with patience and compassion.

Recovery, to me, means:

- Letting my husband really know me, and experiencing his love and acceptance
- Taking the risk to give my husband my full love and trust
- Uncensored prayers and faith that God listens and responds
- Giving birth to my son and gaining a whole new appreciation for what my body can do
- Getting angry when a nurse implied that I'd gained too much weight during my pregnancy, but talking it through with a friend, and then eating and enjoying a piece of my birthday cake anyway
- Setting a goal for myself to live my life so that no one erroneously thinks that I have it all together

- Reminding myself that if I'm not failing, I'm not taking enough risks
- Seeing my body strengthen, not decline, as I gain new experiences
- Believing that my body tells a story, including the story of my son
- Being clothed with strength and dignity, and being able to laugh at the days to come
- Freeing myself from the oppression of perfectionism
- Participating in life rather than just observing it
- Looking forward in hopeful anticipation and looking back with thankfulness and forgiveness, but staying alive and engaged right here in the present as much as possible

Ten years ago, I would never have thought that *alive* and *engaged* would be descriptors for my life. I believe that God guided my path to recovery in small steps, a little bit at a time. I now lead a discussion group at our church where people talk about the hard questions of faith, struggles, doubts, and spiritual truths in a really open and accepting way. Recovery has become a reality to me, and it is my fervent prayer for others to find such richness in life as well.

Mark: Rejecting the Restrictive Mind-set

Mark Warren, MD, is the medical director of the Cleveland Center for Eating Disorders in Ohio. Mark struggled with anorexia in the 1970s, a time when few doctors knew about eating disorders in women, let alone in men. Although he wasn't diagnosed at the time, he later realized that for nearly ten years he'd had the same symptoms as the patients he now treats. Reflecting on his own history, he concludes that full recovery is a gradual process of loosening up and opening outward.

As I've turned away from the restrictive mind-set, life satisfaction and joy have opened up for me. I suspect that the source of this part of my healing has been a dance between community, experience, and acceptance.

My most important therapy was group. In this context I was finally able to take in how others saw me and to make external reality a core part of my world. From this I've been able to build, participate in, and enjoy a true community—people who support my health and happiness, not my eating disorder. This world gives me a reason to be, to live, to figure out what I actually care about. It takes me away from being self-centered. In my world now, I feel loved for who I am—first by my wife (who also taught me to eat well) and by many others in concentric circles around me.

I've learned that I do best when I focus on experience—doing, not thinking. When I'm lost in thought, I rarely feel at my best. When I take action, life gets better. This may mean talking to someone, playing squash, working for the ACLU, taking a guitar lesson, or going out to dinner with friends. Experience makes me feel fulfilled.

Acceptance is my lifelong task. I now understand that so many of the things I thought were mystical aphorisms—"You can't change the past," "There is only now," "Every moment counts," "Love conquers all"—are actually statements of reality. I have days when I'm overwhelmed by how good things are. In these moments, and even those much less overwhelming, I can envision myself as a whole, real person of varied texture who's doing just fine.

The gift of the eating disorder was the entrée to self-discovery. I had to stop my life and look for experience, therapy, and love. I had to accept who I really was and what I needed to do to be happy, healthy, and productive. I stay in recovery because I've been able to make these things core to my everyday life.

Peach: Pregnancy Peace

Peach Friedman, now a yoga teacher, is the author of Diary of an Exercise Addict. *She had recently married and was pregnant when she wrote about the transformation that recovery has brought to her life, her family, and—on a daily basis—to her body.*

MY BELLY IS GROWING. I just sit back and watch it happen. It's out of my control. In the past, this would have been upsetting, but now it's fascinating. There's really a baby in there? My husband and I can't quite believe it. I keep saying to him, "Honey, I know how babies are made, but seriously, how did this happen?" The most basic of human experiences are sometimes the most profound.

I had anorexia eight years ago. I didn't hate my body, I just numbed it. Today I come home on hot summer evenings to find my husband sitting naked on the couch eating a snack. He rides his bike to work and is so hot when he gets home (Sacramento summers are brutal!) that he can't help but disrobe. I join him. We snack on cheese and crackers and watch the news for a little while, to decompress.

I'm new to married life and brand-new to pregnancy, but I love both experiences. OK, let me be a little more honest: they are, so far, two of the hardest things I've ever done. Pregnancy, while celebratory, is a touch uncomfortable. Sometimes more than a touch: I've cursed my changing body a time or two—not because of weight gain (which there has been!) or because of my clothes not fitting (which they no longer do!), and not even because it's out of my control (which it so completely is . . .) but because some days I barely have the energy to get out of bed. Plus, my nipples may never be the same.

Still, I sit back and watch it happen. Eight years ago I could never have managed such enormous change. Eight years ago I probably would have terminated the pregnancy. I take that back: eight years ago I couldn't even kiss a man and enjoy it, let alone have sex and conceive a child! Not to mention, eight years ago I didn't have a menstrual cycle. My body wasn't even a woman's body. I look at the Peach eight years ago, her long skinny body beating away at the pavement in her running shoes, and I imagine what she might think if she saw the Peach of today, round and flushed, naked on the couch with her husband eating cheese on a hot summer evening: *I've let down my guard.* Yes, and this is precisely what lets me love being a new wife and mother.

I love it, not despite the discomforts but including the discomforts. My husband challenges me every day. This growing child inside my flesh challenges me every day. And I do not fight it. I move forward, I take honest steps to care for myself as best I can, given nausea, fatigue—and strange new nipples!

Is Recovery Really Possible?
What Research Tells Us

By Pamela K. Keel

Research in the field of eating disorders bears out the larger truths reflected in the letters in this book. And the most important of these truths is that *recovery does exist.*

Studies show that approximately 75 percent of people who struggle with these disorders are free of ED ten years after the onset of their illness. Of these, approximately 70 percent will not relapse. This means that a majority of people with eating disorders recover fully and for good.

One of my core concerns in researching long-term outcomes has been to identify factors that determine the speed and extent of recovery. Having interviewed many of the participants in my studies, I draw hope from both my research observations and their words:

- *Treatment can help people recover faster,* and those who improve rapidly in treatment tend to have a better overall outcome. However, most people who recover do *not* fall within a "rapid response" group. So, while a positive early response to treatment is an excellent sign, it's in no way a "requirement" for recovery.
- *If you don't use drugs or alcohol, you'll likely have an easier time recovering from an eating disorder.* Studies show, for example, that the absence of drug or alcohol problems is associated with higher remission among those recovering from bulimia.
- *The better the quality of your relationships, the more likely it is that you'll recover without relapsing.* This is true for all eating disorders. In the process of doing my research, I heard many participants emphasize the importance of honesty with themselves and others, and of their faith in helping them break ED's hold on their lives.
- From my work, I have drawn the personal conclusion that *people are stronger than their eating disorder.* Once recovered, most

people reconnect with the person they were before ED. They recognize that ED is something that happened to them and that it may have shaped them, but it was never who they really were. Recovery means separating and reclaiming your true self from ED.

Jenni: Recovered!

Jenni Schaefer is a singer/songwriter, speaker, and author of two best-selling books, Life Without Ed *and* Goodbye Ed, Hello Me. *For some twenty years Jenni struggled with anorexia and bulimia. Those days are long gone.*

"CAN YOU EVER BE RECOVERED from an eating disorder, or are you always in recovery?" I am often asked.

Because I am a speaker and writer in the field of eating disorders, people sometimes believe that I have the answer to every question. I don't, but I do know what is true for my personal battle with anorexia and bulimia. When I wrote *Life Without Ed*, I was in recovery from my eating disorder, so people who've read the book tend to believe that I'm still in that place. But I'm thrilled to say that my recovery journey did not end with *Life Without Ed.*

I no longer walk on eggshells around food. I do not fear relapsing. I've even been through several stressful events in my life—a broken wedding engagement, a family member's battle with cancer, losing my friend to anorexia—and never, not once, considered turning back to eating-disordered behaviors.

I can honestly say that I love my new, healthy body. (Yes, I said *love*!) Thanks to my battle against my own eating disorder, when I hear the societal message that tells us we need to be thinner, I know the truth, and respond accordingly. I focus on health and am grateful for what my body does for me rather than for what it looks like.

Health insurance companies tell us that we're recovered when we eat a specific number of calories per day and when we weigh a certain number on the scale. But being recovered is about much more than any number. It's about seeking balance, having a voice, and letting go of perfection. It's about letting go of the fear of judgment from others. It's about functioning in society and living life to its fullest.

A day in my life looks much different today than it did years ago. Each morning, I spend quiet time in prayer, meditation, and reflection—realizing that a healthy spirituality plays a vital role in my overall health. At night, I give my body plenty of rest. I take time to have fun every day and no longer believe that enjoying myself is a waste of time. I continually uncover lost passions and discover new ones. I finally took my guitar out from the back of my closet, and after ten years, am taking lessons. I bought a mountain bike and am learning a new activity with new friends. I treasure my relationships with friends, family members, and the men I go out with on dates from time to time (even the bad dates).

I experience joy, peace, and love. No longer stuffing and starving feelings with food, I also experience a wide array of other emotions. I sometimes feel sad or angry, which, strangely, signifies huge progress in my life.

I realize that life is a journey, and I engage in personal-growth work to become the best person I can be (not a perfect person). It took almost ten years for me to get to this point of freedom. I can't pinpoint the exact month or even the year that it happened. What I can say for certain is that after making the leap from being in recovery to being recovered, it became important for me to claim it.

Looking back, I can see that as long as I kept referring to myself as being in recovery from my eating disorder, I was giving the illness a place in my life. As long as I believed my eating disorder would haunt me, it did.

So I finally stopped believing it. And I started believing in something else:

I am recovered.

Acknowledgments and
List of Contributors

THIS BOOK TRULY HAS BEEN a labor of love involving hundreds of individuals and countless hours of work over several years—all of it donated for the benefit of the fight against eating disorders. I'm delighted at long last to have the formal opportunity to thank those who helped me bring these pages to fruition.

I could have asked for no more generous, enthusiastic, or discerning partner in this venture than Judith Banker, who saw the need for and value of this book long before she had any hard evidence that it would ever see publication. She's been both brilliant and tireless in writing, reading, revising, collecting, and organizing whatever material was required to make the book come true, and her professional insights were invaluable in highlighting the aspects of recovery that matter most. I often felt guilty for pulling her away from her patients, family, and other duties as president and board member of the Academy for Eating Disorders, but I couldn't have completed this book without her, and I am honored to count her among my friends.

Backing up Judith on this project were the Ann Arbor "G Team" (G for *Gaining*). The incomparable Amanda Weishuhn, MA, chaired the team, which included Kristine Tippen Vazzano, PhD, and Erin Zaleski, MA. Valuable feedback on the manuscript was provided by Kate Fawcett, Kortni Meyers, and Jennifer Lambarth. And backing me up at the keyboard was the fabulous photographer, writer, and technological wizard Alexandra Asher Sears. Thank you all!

I'd be remiss if I didn't also mention my dear friend and fellow author Ellen Graf, who turned this project in a wonderful new direction when she put me in touch with her editor, Eden Steinberg, at Trumpeter Books. Eden's immediate embrace of the project infused us all with the best possible energy. It's been a joy to work on this book with Eden. I've appreciated her grace, her professionalism, and the honest inquiry she's brought to our exchanges.

As we move ahead, I have to thank Donna Friedman, who has graciously volunteered to lead the AED's promotional campaign to launch this book so that it can become an enduring source of hope and information for readers and of revenue and pride for the Academy for Eating Disorders for years to come. I look forward to many events together!

Finally, on a personal note, through the hours, months, and years spent writing and editing this and all my other books, I've had three outstanding men in my life whose support has made every step lighter, more rewarding, and more fun. Props to Marty, Daniel, and Graham. I love you beyond words.

Contributors

I wish I could personally thank each and every person who contributed a letter or article for this book. To those of you whose letters we were unable to include in this collection, I want you to know that you nevertheless made a significant contribution to the project. I hope you can recognize the spirit of your journey in these pages, if not the exact particulars of your story, and I thank you for entrusting me with your reflections.

To those of you whose letters appear in these pages but who preferred to be identified only by first name or pseudonym, I send my heartfelt gratitude for your generosity, your wisdom, and your candor. With equal appreciation, I am pleased to acknowledge the following letter contributors, who granted me permission to use their full names, and the members of the AED who contributed the professional sidebars throughout the book.

LETTERS

STEPHANIE COVINGTON ARMSTRONG is the author of *Not All Black Girls Know How to Eat* and a contributor to the anthology *The Black Body*. She lives in Los Angeles with her husband and three daughters. Her Web site is www.notallblackgirls.com.

BRITTANY LEES BALDWIN was born in southern California and grew up in northern California along with her two identical triplet sisters and three older brothers. She attended Brigham Young University, where she earned a degree in Elementary Education. She currently resides in Texas with her husband and children.

RHONDA BOURNE is a fifty-three-year-old married psychiatric social worker who lives west of Boston with her spouse, beautiful daughter, three dogs, four chickens, and a pond of fish. She is happy more days than not.

REAGAN M. BUSH lives in Dunwoody, Georgia, with her supportive fiancé, Ryan, and their four rescued animals.

GILLIAN CALIG, currently a college student, has been suffering from life-threatening anorexia nervosa for twelve years and is currently attempting to recover.

LAUREN CALIG is a mother, wife, National Eating Disorders Association (NEDA) star member, learning specialist, diversity coordinator, and author.

SARA DUNCAN currently resides in New York City and is continuing to pursue her dream of being an educator through her work as doctoral student at Teachers College, Columbia University.

JULIE DWYER is currently a licensed independent social worker in the state of Ohio.

MICHELE FARRELL-AZUTA is an information technology manager and poet living in downtown Detroit.

ANOUSKA MAREE FIRTH lives in Perth, Australia. Her advice: "Recovery is possible. Make the initial decision to want to get better and start acting like you are. It's possible. I did it. Finally!"

PEACH FRIEDMAN is the author of *Diary of an Exercise Addict.* She is also an eating-disorders educator and yoga teacher. Her Web site is www .peachfriedman.com.

BRIDGET FULLER is a graduate student interested in feminism, activism, and social justice. She is happy to be in recovery so that she can focus on making a positive impact on the amazing world around her, instead of making a negative impact on her body!

ERIN GATES is a Boston-based interior and fashion stylist, freelance writer, and creator of www.elementsofstyleblog.com.

ELA HARRISON GORDON has trained in literature, music, and marriage. She's worked as an academic, chef, beekeeper, farmworker, editor, writer, and translator. She grew up in England and has lived in California, Hawaii, and now Alaska, where she writes and homesteads. She has always been a poet. Ela blogs at www. ulteriorharmony.blogspot.com.

KATIE GREEN is a freelance illustrator based in Bristol, UK. She makes and self-publishes limited-edition books and artwork, as well as designing toys, jewelry, and stationery. She has a degree in Biology and another one in Sequential Illustration, and quite a reputation for baking cakes. Her graphic memoir, tentatively titled *Lighter Than My Shadow* is forthcoming from Jonathan Cape in the UK. Find out more about Katie's work at www.katiegreen.co.uk.

WHITNEY HASSELL is a Christian and communications specialist in Washington, D.C. Her passions are world travel, writing, and meeting new people. She enjoys reading her Bible, taking pictures, and going to the Old Town Alexandria farmer's market. She blogs at www.quickwhit .blogspot.com.

NICOLE HAVEKOST is an artist, parent, wife, and friend.

SHEILA HIMMEL and her daughter, LISA HIMMEL, are the authors of *Hungry: A Mother and Daughter Fight Anorexia*. Lisa is a graduate of the University of California at Santa Cruz with a degree in American Studies. She lives in the Bay Area and hopes to go into social work. Sheila Himmel is an award-winning food critic, writer, and editor. She has written for the *New York Times*, the *Washington Post*, and *USA Today*. Read more about Sheila at www.sheilahimmel.com.

CHERYL KERRIGAN is an author, speaker, and ED survivor. She is the author of *Telling ED NO! and Other Practical Tools to Conquer Your Eating Disorder and Find Freedom* as well as www.getridofed.blogspot.com, a recovery blog. Cheryl "brings recovery to life" by speaking at schools and treatment centers around the country. Her Web site is www.tellingedno.com.

ERIN KROLL is a wedding photo journalist and fine-art photographer. She is passionate about eating-disorder awareness and prevention, and lives in Portland, Maine. Her Web site is www.erinkrollphotography.com.

KIM LAMPSON is a compassionate, dynamic woman whose recovery from anorexia nervosa has made her passionate about her work as a psychologist, author, teacher, and public speaker. In her practice, she counsels people with many different mental disorders and is convinced that there is hope for people who are in emotional pain. You can contact her at www .eatingdisorderssupport.com.

BETH MERCK is a native Texan currently finishing her last semester of nursing school in Dallas. She aspires to be a professional RN specializing in eating disorder treatment. She enjoys scrapbooking in her free time.

BRENDA OELBAUM identifies as a "fat feminist-activist artist," currently working on an installation that confronts the multibillion-dollar diet industry. She is the Michigan representative for the Feminist Art Project, and vice president of the

Midwest Region and president of the Michigan Chapter of the National Women's Caucus for Art. Brenda blogs at www.fatfeministactivistartist.wordpress.com.

JESSIE PETERSON is living life to the fullest in Alaska, where she has been healthy, strong, and out of treatment for over two years. Gathering wild blueberries, climbing mountains with her bulldog, and reading good books are inspiring, rich components of daily life.

AMY PETTENGILL's life and recovery have been an ongoing journey. She would like to thank her mentors, MB, Jodi, Jenni, and Jules; her team members, Tina, Marni, Dorothy, Amy, Thom, Walden, and Castlewood; and her true friends who never let her walk alone. "You all taught me never to stop dreaming or believing."

KATIE PLATT currently lives with her husband and son in Bend, Oregon. She continues to raise awareness of eating disorders in her community and hopes to help with local support groups.

STELLA PORTO is a native Brazilian from Rio de Janeiro. She is married with two sons. She has been living in the United States since 2000, when she relocated with her young family. She currently works as a professor and higher-education administrator, with a special focus in online learning.

JENNI SCHAEFER is a singer/songwriter, speaker, and author of *Life Without Ed: How One Woman Declared Independence from Her Eating Disorder and How You Can Too* and *Goodbye Ed, Hello Me: Recover from Your Eating Disorder and Fall in Love with Life*. Appointed to the Ambassador Council of the National Eating Disorders Association, she is also a consultant with Center for Change in Orem, Utah. Visit her Web site at www.JenniSchaefer.com.

ANGELA SCHAFFNER struggled with anorexia and bulimia in college. Now thirty-three, she's a psychologist at the Atlanta Center for Eating Disorders, an outpatient treatment center in Atlanta, Georgia. For Angela, recovery is an ongoing act of faith. You can contact her at www.angelaschaffnerphd.com.

LAURA CARIM TODD is a scientist unraveling the human mind, a certified yoga teacher, a proud wife to David, and the mother of an inspiring ten-month-old daughter. She keeps ED at bay, learning who she is and loving life for what it is: a unique opportunity to fully *be*.

SIDEBARS

DIANN M. ACKARD, PhD, LP, FAED (USA), is a licensed psychologist and consultant who serves on the faculty of the University of Minnesota. A former member of the Board of Directors of the Academy for Eating Disorders (AED), she also maintains a private practice in Minneapolis. She conducts research on trauma and eating disorders and is cochair of the AED Trauma Special Interest Group. For further information visit www.diannackard.com.

JUDITH D. BANKER, MA, LLP, FAED (USA), is Founder and Executive Director of the Center for Eating Disorders, a nonprofit support and outpatient treatment facility in Ann Arbor, Michigan, established in 1983. She lectures internationally and has published on the clinical treatment of eating disorders and on methods for bridging research and practice. She is Past President and a Fellow of the Academy for Eating Disorders. For further information visit www.center4ed.org and www.stopcompulsiveeating.com.

OVIDIO BERMUDEZ, MD, FAED (USA), is Medical Director of Child and Adolescent Services at Eating Recovery Center in Denver, Colorado. He serves as Clinical Professor of Psychiatry and Pediatrics at the University of Oklahoma College of Medicine and is Board-certified in Pediatrics and Adolescent Medicine. Dr. Bermudez is a Fellow of the Academy for Eating Disorders (AED), the Society for Adolescent Medicine, and the American Academy of Pediatrics. He chairs the AED Medical Care Special Interest Group and the AED Hispano Latino American Chapter, and serves as Cochair of the Medical Care Standards Task Force. For further information visit www.eatingrecoverycenter.com.

WAYNE A. BOWERS, PhD, FAED (USA), is Clinical Professor and Director of the Eating Disorder Program in the Department of Psychiatry at the University of Iowa. Dr. Bowers has been working and writing in the field of eating disorders since 1988, focusing mainly on the use of cognitive therapy in the treatment of eating disorders. He was trained in cognitive therapy with Aaron Beck and is a Fellow of the Academy for Eating Disorders and Academy of Cognitive Therapy.

CYNTHIA M. BULIK, PhD, FAED (USA), is the William and Jeanne Jordan Distinguished Professor of Eating Disorders in the Department of Psychiatry at the School of Medicine and Professor of Nutrition in the School of Public Health at the University of North Carolina–Chapel Hill. Past President of the Academy for Eating Disorders and Director of the University of North Carolina Eating Disorders Program, Dr. Bulik has published more than 350 scientific papers and chapters on eating disorders. Her most recent book is *Crave: Why You Binge Eat and How to Stop* (Walker). Her research includes treatment, laboratory, epidemiological, and genetic studies of eating disorders. For further information visit www.unceatingdisorders.org (program Web site); www.uncexchanges.wordpress.com (program blog); and www.cravethebook.com.

Deb Burgard, PhD (USA), is a psychologist specializing in eating and body-image concerns across the weight spectrum. She is one of the founding proponents of the Health at Every Size (HAES) model, coauthor of the Academy for Eating Disorder's (AED) "Guidelines for Childhood Obesity Prevention Programs," Cochair of AED's HAES Special Interest Group, and creator of BodyPositive.com. Her most recent publications include chapters in *The Fat Studies Reader,* edited by Esther Rothblum and Sondra Solovay; *Effective Clinical Practice in the Treatment of Eating Disorders: The Heart of the Matter,* edited by Margo Maine, William N. Davis, and Jane Shure; and *Treatment of Eating Disorders: Bridging the Research-Practice Gap,* edited by Margo Maine, Beth Hartman McGilley, and Douglas Bunnell. She maintains a private practice in Los Altos, California. For further information visit www.bodypositive.com.

Rachel M. Calogero, PhD (UK/USA), is Assistant Professor of Psychology at Virginia Wesleyan College in Norfolk, Virginia. She earned a PhD in Social Psychology at the University of Kent in Canterbury, U.K., and completed a postdoctoral research fellowship at the University of Kent in the School of Psychology. She conducts research and gives talks internationally on the role of sexual and self-objectification in the lives of girls and women, the role of exercise in eating-disorders treatment and recovery, and the perpetuation of sexism and fat prejudice. She has published her research widely in peer-reviewed journals and book chapters, and is senior editor of the book *Self-Objectification in Women: Causes, Consequences, and Counteractions* (APA, 2010).

Myra J. Cooper, DPhil (UK), is Senior Research Tutor at the University of Oxford, Doctoral Course in Clinical Psychology, and Senior Research Fellow at Harris Manchester College at the University of Oxford. She is a clinical psychologist by profession. Her interests in the field of eating disorders include cognitive and emotional processing, self and identity, and cognitive and meta-cognitive therapy.

Scott Crow, MD, FAED (USA), is a graduate of the University of Minnesota Medical School and its Psychiatry Residency Training Program, where he was Chief Resident and a Consult-Liaison Psychiatry Fellow. His research interests include the causes, course, and treatment of eating disorders. He is a Past President and a Fellow of the Academy for Eating Disorders. He has received a midcareer Independent Scientist Award from NIMH focused on the treatment of eating disorders. He is currently Director of the Midwest Regional Postdoctoral Training Program in Eating Disorders Research, as well as Director of the Disordered-Eating/Assessment Core of the Minnesota Obesity Center.

ANGELA CELIO DOYLE, PhD (USA), is a licensed clinical psychologist at the University of Chicago's Eating and Weight Disorders Program. After earning her bachelor and master's degrees at Stanford University, Dr. Doyle received her PhD from the University of California at San Diego. Dr. Doyle has published more than sixty scholarly articles, abstracts, and book chapters on the prevention and treatment of eating disorders in youth as well as the use of the Internet for health promotion, and has presented her work at national and international conferences.

THERESA FASSIHI, PhD (USA), is Cofounder of the Houston Eating- Disorders Center, which provides intensive outpatient treatment for eating disorders using a treatment-team approach and evidence-based interventions. As a former journalist, she is committed to advocacy work to educate the public and raise awareness of the need for adequate access to treatment for patients and their families. She is Cochair of the Advocacy and Communications Committee for the Academy for Eating Disorders. Previously, she has worked in inpatient and outpatient eating-disorder treatment settings in the United Kingdom and at the Menninger Clinic, and continues to serve as Assistant Professor with Baylor College of Medicine.

ANGELA FAVARO, MS, PhD (Italy), has a PhD in Psychiatric Sciences (University of Verona) and a Master of Science in Genetic Epidemiology (International Master School of University of Pavia). She is a researcher and Professor at the School of Medicine, University of Padua, in Italy. In addition she is a psychotherapist specializing in the treatment of people with eating disorders. She has published a number of papers in the areas of epidemiology, self-injurious behavior, response to treatment, and risk factors in eating disorders.

JOSIE GELLER, PhD (British Columbia), is Associate Professor in the Department of Psychiatry at the University of British Columbia and Director of Research for the Eating Disorders Program at St. Paul's Hospital in British Columbia. Dr. Geller's clinical and research interests focus on understanding readiness and motivation for change in the assessment and treatment of individuals with eating disorders, and she has expanded her work to other populations, including HIV, substance use, and obesity. Her program of research aims to provide a set of guiding principles for efficient, cost-effective care. She has published extensively and is an internationally renowned speaker.

BETH HARTMAN MCGILLEY PhD, FAED (USA), is a psychologist in private practice in Wichita, Kansas, specializing in the treatment of eating and related disorders, body image, athletes and sports performance, trauma, and grief. A Fellow of the Academy for Eating Disorders, Dr. McGilley has practiced psychotherapy for twenty-five years in addition to writing, lecturing, supervising, and developing and directing an inpatient eating-disorders program. She is an editor for *Eating Disorders: The Journal of Treatment and Prevention*, and coeditor with Margo Maine and Doug Bunnell of the book, *Treatment of Eating Disorders: Bridging the Research-Practice Gap*. For further information about this book visit www .elsevierdirect.com/product.jsp?isbn=9780123756688.

TOM HILDEBRANDT, PsyD (USA), is Director of the Eating and Weight Disorders Program at Mount Sinai School of Medicine in New York. A clinical psychologist, Dr. Hildebrandt has served as the Cochair of the Academy for Eating Disorders, Males, and Eating—Disorders Special-Interest Group since 2005 and has received several grants from the National Institutes of Health to study men who use appearance and performance-enhancing drugs. He is an expert in the treatment and study of body-image disturbances.

NURAY O. KANBUR, MD (Turkey), is an Associate Professor of Pediatrics in the Faculty of Medicine and Division of Adolescent Medicine, Department of Pediatrics at Hacettepe University. Dr. Kanbur graduated from Hacettepe University, Faculty of Medicine, and completed her residency there in the Department of Pediatrics. She completed her clinical fellowship in the Division of Adolescent Medicine at The Hospital for Sick Children in Toronto, Canada. She is a clinician and researcher in the Division of Adolescent Medicine at Hacettepe University. Her research and publications are in a variety of areas of adolescent medicine.

DEBRA K. KATZMAN, MD, FAED (Canada), is Professor of Pediatrics and Head of the Division of Adolescent Medicine in the Department of Pediatrics at the University of Toronto. She is also the Medical Director of the Eating Disorders Program and Senior Associate Scientist at the Research Institute at the Hospital for Sick Children. Dr. Katzman's research focuses on the unique medical complications associated with pediatric eating disorders, in particular osteoporosis and amenorrhea, and the role of brain structure and function in eating disorders. Dr. Katzman has published over a hundred articles, abstracts, book chapters, and editorials, and is an associate editor for *Adolescent Health Care: A Practical Guide*, 5th edition and coeditor of *Help for Eating Disorders: A Parent's Guide to Symptoms, Causes and Treatments*. She also lectures nationally and internationally on the medical complications of child- and adolescent-onset eating disorders. Dr. Katzman is the 2010–2011 President and a Fellow of the Academy for Eating Disorders.

PAMELA K. KEEL, PhD, FAED (USA), is Professor of Psychology at Florida State University. She received her PhD in Clinical Psychology from the University of

Minnesota. Dr. Keel conducts NIH-funded research on the nosology, epidemiology, and longitudinal course of bulimic syndromes and has published over a hundred articles and authored two books on eating disorders. Current Treasurer of the AED Board of Directors, she was elected as an AED fellow in 2006 and served as 2009–2010 President for the Eating Disorders Research Society. Dr. Keel is on the editorial board of the *International Journal of Eating Disorders* and is an Associate Editor of the *Journal of Abnormal Psychology.*

YAEL LATZER, Dsc (Israel), is Associate Professor of Social Welfare and Health Sciences and head of the Clinical Program at the School of Social Work at Haifa University in Haifa, Israel. She is Founder and Director of the Eating Disorders (ED) Clinic at Rambam Medical Center and a founder and incoming President of the Israeli Association for Eating Disorders. She is a member of the Academy for Eating Disorders and the Eating Disorders Research Society. Professor Latzer has authored and coauthored more than seventy papers in peer-reviewed journals as well as twenty-eight book chapters, and has edited a book on eating disorders.

PAM MACDONALD (UK) is a PhD student working on a DVD skills-based training project at the Institute of Psychiatry, London. She worked with Janet Treasure and Ulrike Schmidt in editing the book *The Clinician's Guide to Collaborative Caring in Eating Disorders: The New Maudsley Method.* She also supports family members by coaching them using the principles of motivational interviewing.

JOHN F. MORGAN, MA, MD, FRCPsych, FHEA (UK), is Medical Director of the Yorkshire Centre for Eating Disorders in Leeds. He is Visiting Professor at Leeds Metropolitan University and Senior Lecturer in Eating Disorders at St Georges, University of London, where he runs a national research network. He is Vice-chair of the Royal College of Psychiatrists' Eating Disorders Section and a member of the Academy for Eating Disorders, as well as a member of the Eating Disorders Research Society. For more information about Dr. Morgan visit www.psychiatry-uk.org.

BOB PALMER, FRCPsych, FAED (UK), serves as editor of the *European Eating Disorders Review,* Honorary Professor at Leicester University, and Consultant Psychiatrist for the Leicester Adult Eating Disorders Service (Leicestershire Partnership NHS Trust). A highly regarded researcher, clinician, and writer, he has authored numerous research and clinical articles, three books, and edited two others. His contributions to the Academy for Eating Disorders (AED) and to the field earned Professor Palmer the 2005 AED Leadership Award for Clinical, Educational, and Administrative Service and the AED 2010 Lifetime Achievement

Award. He is now semiretired and for the first time in forty-four years is no longer seeing patients.

SUSAN J. PAXTON, PhD, FAED (Aus.), is Professor and Head of the School of Psychological Science, La Trobe University, Australia. Professor Paxton has a long-standing interest in the issues of prevention, risk factors, and early intervention for body-image and eating disorders. She is Past President of the Australian and New Zealand Academy for Eating Disorders and is Past President and a Fellow of the Academy for Eating Disorders. She has also been a member of the National Ministerial Advisory Group on Body Image in Australia. For further information visit www.latrobe.edu.au/psy/staff/paxtons.html.

AMY PERSHING, LMSW (USA), is Clinical Director of the Center for Eating Disorders and Founding Director of the Bodywise Binge Eating Disorder Treatment Program of the Center for Eating Disorders in Ann Arbor, Michigan, and Annapolis, Maryland. Amy Pershing has lectured nationally and been featured on both radio and television on BED treatment and the Health at Every Size (HAES) paradigm. She is a board member of the Binge Eating Disorder Association (BEDA), a member of the Academy for Eating Disorders (AED), and a member of the AED Health at Every Size (HAES) Special Interest Group. For further information visit www.stopcompulsiveeating.com and www.center4ed.org.

SUSAN RINGWOOD (UK) has served as Chief Executive of beat, the United Kingdom's largest eating-disorders charity, since 2002. She was a member of the National Institute of Health and Clinical Excellence (NICE) Guideline Development Group for Eating Disorders, and is a lay member of the NICE consideration panel for Mental Health. She is a member of the advisory board of the Academy of Eating Disorders and is Cochair of the Academy's Patient and Carers Task Force. She was the 2008 recipient of the AED Meehan-Hartley Award for Public Service and Advocacy. Susan Ringwood is a member of the Royal College of Psychiatrists Eating Disorders section Executive Committee. For further information visit www.b-eat.co.uk.

LUCY SERPELL, DClinPsy (UK), is an Honorary Clinical Psychologist at North East London Foundation NHS Trust and a lecturer at University College London. With more than fifteen years' experience working with people with eating disorders, her interests include eating disorders research focused on cognition, motivation, and personality in anorexia nervosa. She also studies the neuropsychology of perseverative behavior in eating disorders. Part of this research explores letters written by people with eating disorders. She is a member of the Academy for Eating Disorders.

BETH SHELTON, DPsych (Aus.), works as a clinician, consultant, and educator in the areas of eating disorders, body image and movement. At MonashLink Community Health Service, Dr. Shelton has developed a disordered-eating service, which provides early-accessible and multidisciplinary treatment for eating disorders and obesity. She also works at the Centre of Excellence in Eating Disorders, a statewide service providing support, training, and consultation in eating-disorders treatment to clinicians in the public health sector. Beth Shelton is associated with Susan Paxton's research team at La Trobe University and is a member of the executive board of the Australia and New Zealand Academy of Eating Disorders. A psychologist with a professional background in choreography and community cultural development, she uses creative movement and dance in group interventions for disordered eating and body dissatisfaction.

MARY TANTILLO, PhD, RN, FAED (USA), is Director of the Western New York Comprehensive Care Center for Eating Disorders, Associate Professor of Clinical Nursing at the University of Rochester School of Nursing, and Clinical Associate Professor in the Department of Psychiatry at the University of Rochester School of Medicine in Rochester, New York. Dr. Tantillo is a Fellow of the Academy for Eating Disorders, a former AED board member, and present Chair of the AED Credentialing Task Force and Cochair of the Patient and Carers Task Force. Additionally, Dr. Tantillo is the CEO/Clinical Director of The Healing Connection, LLC, an eating-disorders partial-hospitalization program in Fairport, New York. Dr. Tantillo is the recipient of the AED's 2010 Meehan-Hartley Award for Public Service and Advocacy. For further information visit www.nyeat ingdisorders.org.

JANET TREASURE, FRPsych, FAED (UK), is Professor of Psychiatry at King's College and Head of the Eating Disorders Unit at the South London and Maudsley NHS Trust. Professor Treasure is a Fellow of the Academy for Eating Disorders. In 2004 she was awarded the AED's Leadership Award for Research. As well as editing professional texts, she has written several self-help books for people with eating disorders and their care givers in order to share her expertise and understanding. Further details of her team's research are available at www. eatingresearch.com.

EVELYN TRIBOLE, MS, RD (USA), has written seven books and coauthored the book *Intuitive Eating: A Revolutionary Program That Works*. She maintains a private practice specializing in eating disorders in Newport Beach, California, and teaches Intuitive Eating PRO skills to health professionals. She received the American Dietetic Association's award for Excellence in Private Practice. She is a renowned speaker and educator on the topics of intuitive eating and nutrition. For further visit www.EvelynTribole.com.

KRISTIN VON RANSON, PhD, FAED (Canada), is Associate Professor of Psychology at the University of Calgary in Alberta, Canada. A registered psychologist, she is a member of the Eating Disorders Research Society and a Fellow of the Academy for Eating Disorders. She received her doctorate in Clinical Psychology from the University of Minnesota and completed pre-doctoral internship training at Western Psychiatric Institute and Clinic in Pittsburgh, Pennsylvania, and a post-doctoral fellowship at Cincinnati Children's Hospital Medical Center. Dr. von Ranson has published twenty-five articles and book chapters on a range of topics related to eating disorders and body image.

MARK WARREN, MD, MPH, FAED (USA), is Medical Director at the Cleveland Center for Eating Disorders in Cleveland, Ohio. Dr. Warren is a graduate of the Johns Hopkins University Medical School and completed his residency at Harvard Medical School. He served as Chairman of the Department of Psychiatry at Mount Sinai Hospital in Cleveland. A past Vice-chair for Clinical Affairs at the Case School of Medicine Department of Psychiatry, he continues on the clinical faculty of the medical school, teaching in the departments of both Psychiatry and Pediatrics. He is a Fellow of the Academy for Eating Disorders and leads the Males and Eating Disorders Special Interest Group for the Academy for Eating Disorders. Dr. Warren is a Distinguished Fellow of the American Psychiatric Association, a two-time recipient of the Exemplary Psychiatrist Award of the National Alliance for the Mentally Ill, and a winner of the Woodruff Award. For further information visit www.eatingdisordersc-leveland.org.

KITTY WESTIN, MA, LP (USA), began her work in advocacy ten years ago after her daughter, Anna Westin, died from anorexia. She and her family founded the Anna Westin Foundation in 2000 (now the Emily Program Foundation), and since then she has spoken to millions of people about the seriousness of eating disorders. Kitty Westin is the current president of the Emily Program Foundation. She is active in the Eating Disorders Coalition and has been a member of the board for nine years. She cochairs the AED Advocacy Communications Committee and is a member of the Patient and Carers Task Force. For further information about the Eating Disorders Coalition visit www.eatingdisorderscoalition.org.

LUCENE WISNIEWSKI, PhD, FAED (USA), is Clinical Director and Cofounder of the Cleveland Center for Eating Disorders and is an Adjunct Assistant Professor of Psychology at Case Western Reserve University. Her research and clinical interests include using empirically founded treatments to inform clinical programs. She provides workshops on the CBT and DBT treatment of eating disorders nationally. Dr. Wisniewski has been elected Fellow and has served on the board of directors of the Academy for Eating Disorders. She is currently coleader of AED's Borderline Personality Disorder Special Interest Group. For further information visit www.eatingdisorderscleveland.org/blog.

Resources

Online Information Sources

- EATING DISORDER HOPE, www.eatingdisorderhope.com
  A source for treatment information and recovery tools
- EATING DISORDER REFERRAL AND INFORMATION CENTER,
  www.edreferral.com
  A source for comprehensive treatment referral information
- EATING DISORDERS TREATMENT HELP, www.edtreatmenthelp.org
  A resource for those advocating for insurance coverage on behalf of individuals with eating disorders
- GÜRZE BOOKS, www.gurze.com
  A publisher and online distributor of books, videos, periodicals, and other information about eating disorders and related therapies
- SOMETHING FISHY, www.somethingfishy.org
  A prorecovery Web site and online forum promoting awareness and support for people with eating disorders

International Eating-Disorders Organizations

THE ACADEMY FOR EATING DISORDERS (AED), www.aedweb.org
An international professional association committed to leadership in eating-disorders research, education, prevention, and treatment. Information about eating disorders and a listing of eating-disorders specialists in your area can be found at www.aedweb.org/About_Eating_Disorders/1857.htm.

Families Empowered and Supporting Treatment of Eating Disorders (FEAST), www.feast-ed.org
An international support, education, and advocacy organization for parents and caregivers.

AED Sister Organizations and Chapters

The AED establishes formal collaborations with regional professional eating-disorders associations around the world who share the AED's mission of promoting the treatment, research, and prevention of eating disorders. Currently these collaborations include the following:

AED Hispano Latino American Chapter, www.aedweb.org

Australia and New Zealand Academy for Eating Disorders (ANZAED), www.anzaed.org.au

Dutch Academy for Eating Disorders (Nederlandse Academie voor Eetstoornissen) (NAE), www.naeweb.nl

Eating Disorders Association of Canada (EDAC), www.edac-atac.ca

Israeli Association for Eating Disorders (IAED), www.iaed.org.il

Mexican Association of Eating Disorders Professionals (Asociación Mexicana de Trastornos Alimentarios) (AMTA), www.izta cala.unam.mx/amta

Transdisciplinary Obesity Society (Sociedad Transdisciplinaria de Obesidad, Argentina) (STO), www.drcormillot.com/sto

Regional Eating-Disorders Organizations Worldwide

United States

Binge Eating Disorder Association (BEDA), www.bedaonline.com *An association for people with Binge Eating Disorder, their families and friends, and treatment professionals.*

Eating Disorders Coalition for Research, Policy, and Action, www.eatingdisorderscoalition.org
A national organization that concentrates on public-health-policy advocacy, lobbying, and awareness.

National Association of Anorexia Nervosa and Associated Disorders (ANAD), www.anad.org
A national network that offers treatment referrals, education, support-group network, conference, and advocacy.

National Eating Disorders Association (NEDA), www.nationaleatingdis orders.org
A national organization that hosts an annual conference and family-and-friends network, and promotes advocacy and public awareness.

Canada

Eating Disorder Resource Centre of British Columbia (EDRCBC), www .disorderedeating.ca
Education, referral, and research services, including resource-counselor help line.

National Eating Disorders Centre (NEDIC), www.nedic.ca
Information and resources on eating disorders and weight preoccupation.

Germany

Eating Disorders Network (Netzwerk Essstörungen), www.netzwerk-esss toerungen.at
Hosts an annual conference and provides training and education.

German Society on Eating Disorders (Deutsche Gesellschaft für Essstörungen), www.dgess.de
A society of eating-disorders research professionals.

Hong Kong

Hong Kong Eating Disorders Association (HEDA), www.heda-hk.org
A family/carer and patient-support, referral, education, and advocacy organization.

Ireland

Bodywhys Eating Disorder Association of Ireland, www.bodywhys.ie
Provides online support and information.

Italy

Italian Society for the Study of Eating Disorders (SIS.DCA), www.dis turbialimentazione.it
Professional society dedicated to the study, prevention, and treatment of eating disorders.

JAPAN

EATING DISORDERS NETWORK OF JAPAN (EDNJ), www.ednetwork.jp
Education, awareness, and prevention organization bringing together research and treatment professionals, families, and sufferers. Hosts annual conference.

SPAIN

ASOCIACIÓN ESPAÑOLA PARA EL ESTUDIO DE LOS TRASTORNOS DE CONDUCTA ALIMENTARIA (AEETCA), www.gonzalomorande.eresmas.net
Association for eating-disorders research and treatment professionals. Hosts a regular conference.

UNITED KINGDOM

BEATING EATING DISORDERS (beat), www.b-eat.co.uk
The leading UK eating-disorders charity, providing information and help on all aspects of eating disorders.

Position Papers and Guidelines from the AED

The AED periodically releases statements and position papers on issues related to eating disorders. The following informational guidelines are all available online at www.aedweb.org/Advocacy/1922.htm:

AED World Wide Charter for Action on Eating Disorders—the patient and family "bill of rights"—outlines the rights and expectations that people with eating disorders and their families can seek from those responsible for health policies and practices worldwide.

Eating Disorders Are Serious Mental Illnesses outlines the position of the AED that anorexia nervosa and bulimia nervosa, along with their variants, are biologically based, serious mental illnesses and warrant the same level and breadth of health care coverage as other mental-health conditions (for example, schizophrenia, bipolar disorder, depression).

Guidelines for Childhood Obesity Prevention Programs provides guidelines to minimize the risk of unintended consequences for obesity prevention programs, for example, negative self-esteem, body dissatisfaction, and eating-disordered behaviors in young people, and the inadvertent reinforcement of stigma.

The Role of the Family in Eating Disorders outlines the AED's position condemning generalizing statements that imply families are to blame for their child's illness.

About the Academy
for Eating Disorders (AED)

THE ACADEMY FOR EATING DISORDERS, formed in 1993, is a global professional association committed to leadership in eating-disorders research, education, treatment, and prevention.

The AED brings together scientists, practitioners, and other key stakeholders from over forty countries on six continents, who are active in eating-disorders research, clinical practice, and advocacy and prevention. The association promotes collaboration and sharing of knowledge about current research findings and initiatives, best practices, treatment innovations, and public and professional education, political action, and awareness efforts. Key AED offerings include the annual AED International Conference on Eating Disorders (ICED), the *International Journal of Eating Disorders*, over twenty special-interest groups, regional and on-line training and education programs, a research-grant and clinical-scholarship program, and an international member Listserv. For further information, visit www.aedweb.org or write to:

The Academy for Eating Disorders
111 Deer Lake Road, Suite 100
Deerfield, Illinois 60015 USA

About Aimee Liu

Aimee Liu is an author and teacher whose last book, *Gaining: The Truth about Life after Eating Disorders*, drew on her own experience as well as interviews with more than forty others with histories of eating disorders. Back in 1979, Liu wrote America's first memoir of anorexia nervosa, *Solitaire*. She is also a novelist. Her fiction includes *Flash House, Cloud Mountain,* and *Face*. These books have been translated into more than a dozen languages.

Aimee Liu is a member of the core faculty in Goddard College's MFA program in creative writing at Port Townsend, Washington. She serves on the advisory boards of the Academy for Eating Disorders and the Philadelphia-based organization A Chance to Heal. She lives with her husband in Los Angeles.

For more information, visit www.gainingthetruth.com.